# Experiencing His Victory

## Seminar Workbook

## Terry L. Tuinder

Experiencing His Victory Publishing
514 N 4th St, Suite 2
Grand Forks, ND 58203

Graphic Design on front Cover by Terry L. Tuinder

Experiencing His Victory Seminar Workbook / Terry L. Tuinder

ISBN 978 - 1 - 79 - 544005 - 9

# Table of Contents

# Week 1

## Examine Your Relationship with God

### This Week's Goals

- To expose faulty views of salvation and place 100% of your faith in the finished work of Christ on the cross.

- To expose faulty views of God and replace them with a true picture of God.

- To boldly choose to repent and turn away from any willful sin in your life.

# Week 1 Teaching Notes

## Foundational Scriptures

Exodus 34:6-7a

6 Then the Lord passed by in front of him and proclaimed, "The Lord, the Lord God, compassionate and gracious, slow to anger, and abounding in lovingkindness and truth; 7 who keeps lovingkindness for thousands,

Psalm 103:1-5

1 Bless the Lord, O my soul,
And all that is within me, bless His holy name.
2 Bless the Lord, O my soul,
And forget none of His benefits;
3 Who pardons all your iniquities,
Who heals all your diseases;
4 Who redeems your life from the pit,
Who crowns you with lovingkindness and compassion;
5 Who satisfies your years with good things,
So that your youth is renewed like the eagle.

John 3:16-18

16 "For God so loved the world, that He gave His only begotten Son, that whoever believes in Him shall not perish, but have eternal life. 17 For God did not send the Son into the world to judge the world, but that the world might be saved through Him. 18 He who believes in Him is not judged; he who does not believe has been judged already, because he has not believed in the name of the only begotten Son of God.

Isaiah 53:4-5

4 Surely our griefs He Himself bore,
And our sorrows He carried;
Yet we ourselves esteemed Him stricken,
Smitten of God, and afflicted.
5 But He was pierced through for our transgressions,
He was crushed for our iniquities;
The chastening for our well-being fell upon Him,
And by His scourging we are healed.

Psalm 103:10-14

10 He has not dealt with us according to our sins,
Nor rewarded us according to our iniquities.
11 For as high as the heavens are above the earth,
So great is His lovingkindness toward those who fear Him.
12 As far as the east is from the west,
So far has He removed our transgressions from us.
13 Just as a father has compassion on his children,
So the Lord has compassion on those who fear Him.
14 For He Himself knows our frame;
He is mindful that we are but dust.

Romans 8:31-37

31 What then shall we say to these things? If God is for us, who is against us? 32 He who did not spare His own Son, but delivered Him over for us all, how will He not also with Him freely give us all things? 33 Who will bring a charge against God's elect? God is the

one who justifies; 34 who is the one who condemns? Christ Jesus is He who died, yes, rather who was raised, who is at the right hand of God, who also intercedes for us. 35 Who will separate us from the love of Christ? Will tribulation, or distress, or persecution, or famine, or nakedness, or peril, or sword? 36 Just as it is written,

"For Your sake we are being put to death all day long;
We were considered as sheep to be slaughtered."

37 But in all these things we overwhelmingly conquer through Him who loved us. 38 For I am convinced that neither death, nor life, nor angels, nor principalities, nor things present, nor things to come, nor powers, 39 nor height, nor depth, nor any other created thing, will be able to separate us from the love of God, which is in Christ Jesus our Lord.

## Faulty Views of Salvation

1. Born into a Christian family/ Baptized as a baby

Romans 10:9-10

2. I'm good enough

3. I follow the rules

John 5:39-40

4. I'm strong enough

Galatians 3:2-3

Prayer for salvation

Father, I come to you on the basis of the shed blood of Jesus Christ. I acknowledge that I have sinned against you and I'm in need of a savior. I reject any effort to save myself. I trust in the death and resurrection of Jesus Christ. Today I choose to repent and turn from my sin to accept Jesus Christ as my Lord and Savior. I ask you to fill me with Your Holy Spirit to empower me to live the Christian life. In Jesus' name, Amen.

## Faulty Views of God

Genesis 3:1-4

Genesis 3:6-7

Good Father

Passive Father

Absent Father

Performance-Orientated Father

Authoritarian Father

Abusive Father

Indulgent Father

Overprotective Father

Good Ole Boy Father

## Willful Sin Against God

Sin always brings forth death

James 1:13-15

God never tempts you

You are tempted by your own desires

Sin is a willful decision to rebel against God's truth and do things your own way

Sin always brings forth separation

Sin hinders your relationship with God and others

Come up with a plan

Psalm 139:23-24

# Class Discussion

**1. What part of the lesson was most important to you? Why?**

Terry mentioned several ways people believe saves them and makes them Christians.

> Being born into a Christian family
> Being baptized as an infant
> Believing that your are good enough
> Believing you are following the right rules
> Believing you are strong enough on your own

**2. Have you ever believed any of these faulty views about salvation or something similar? If so, share which one and how you came to know the truth about God's salvation. (short version, please)**

On the following pages are many faulty views of God. Please look through them and answer the following questions.

**3. Has this teaching revealed any faulty views about God of which you were unaware? If so, how?**

**4. Which of the faulty views of God do you relate to the most? Why?**

**5. Have you overcome any of these faulty views of God in your personal life? If so, how?**

Terry talked about about making a choice to walk away from willful sin in your life. Based on what he said answer the following question.

**6. Is there any area of willful sin in your life that Lord is pointing out right now? (You don't have to share what it is) If yes, are you willing to make a commitment right now to turn from your sin and walk in God's ways?**

# Faulty Views of God

## The Absent God

### Key Concept

God is not with you

### His Characteristics

God is absent

God is disengaged

God is uninvolved

God is unsupportive

God is never there when you need Him

God is uncaring

### Your Responses

You feel depressed

You feel insecure

You feel unloved

You feel abandoned

You feel alone

You feel self-loathing

You feel rejected

You feel responsible

### Key Response

You try to do the best you can

## The Abusive God

### Key Concept

God is cruel to you

### His Characteristics

God is hateful

God is spiteful

Good is critical

God is judgmental

God is demeaning

God is cruel

God is violent

### Your Responses

You feel shamed

You feel embarrassed before friends

You feel angry

You feel belittled

You feel judged

You feel condemned

You feel helpless

### Key Response

You constantly walk on egg shells

# The Angry God

## Key Concept

God is angry with you

## His Characteristics

God hates you

God is always angry at you

God is always judging you

God sits in heaven waiting for you to mess up

God loves punishing you when you mess up

God is mean, cruel, and vindictive

## Your Responses

You feel guilty

You're filled with fear

You have a feeling of dread

You tread on eggshells

You're waiting for God to pour out His wrath on you

You feel like you're a bad or evil person

## Key Response

You seek to hide from God

# The Authoritarian God

## Key Concept

God's way is the only way

## His Characteristics

Demanding like a drill sergeant

Expects instant obedience

Expects perfect behavior

Rule oriented

Harsh disciplinarian

Emotionally cold

Black-and-white thinking

Stiff, Strict

Emotionally Distant

Controlling & Domineering

Always right

## Your Responses

You feel controlled

You feel demeaned

You feel angry

You feel unheard

You feel shamed

You are either passive or aggressive

You either submit or rebel

You feel resentful

You have low self-esteem

You feel insecure

You feel indecisive

## Key Response

You either become quite submissive to avert confrontations or you rebel and buck the system

| The Distant God | The Good Ole Boy God |
|---|---|
| **Key Concept** | **Key Concept** |
| God is far away from you | God's just like you |
| **His Characteristics** | **His Characteristics** |
| God is far from you | God takes care of His own |
| God is aloof | God is unassuming |
| God does not hear you | God is easy going |
| God does not care | God is jovial |
| God is not interested in you | God is your buddy |
| **Your Responses** | **Your Responses** |
| You feel unloved | You treat God like He is just another one of your buddies |
| You feel unimportant | You think that God is just like you |
| You feel alone | You think God winks at your sin |
| You feel abandoned | You think God's got your back no matter what you do |
| You feel hopeless | |
| **Key Response** | **Key Response** |
| You try to be the best you can because you are on your own | You treat God like a buddy rather than Lord |

# The Indulgent God

## Key Concept

God is tolerant of you

## His Characteristics

God is only a God of grace

God forgives all past, present, and future sins so there is no need for repentance

God will not discipline you as a believer

God will not judge you for your actions

God will not send a person to hell

God will ensure that every person is saved because Jesus died for the sins of the world

## Your Responses

You live a sinful life and believe it is okay because all your sins are forgiven

You believe you will not be held responsible for your sins

You believe that any commandments, including the ten commandments, are legalism and can be ignored

## Key Response

You believe you are forgiven no matter what you do

# The Legalistic God

## Key Concept

God is restrictive to you

## His Characteristics

God is legalistic

God weighs you down with so many rules

God restricts your life by taking away everything that is fun

God is a party pooper

God is stuffy and old fashioned

## Your Responses

You struggle with all the rules feeling that they take away all the fun things of life

You feel like going to church, reading the Bible, praying, and tithing are duties that must be performed

You trust that the things that you do ensures your salvation

You become very legalistic in your efforts to serve God and believe that everything must be done a certain way

You make up more rules than God has given to ensure you do things right

## Key Response

You make following the rules the most important thing in your life or you totally give up trying

# The Overprotective God

## Key Concept

God is smothering you

## His Characteristics

God micromanages everything

God must keep you from failing

God doesn't teach responsibility

God is over consoling

God bubble wraps you

God smothers you

God is constantly checking up on you

God is restrictive

God is always warning of danger

## Your Responses

You feel smothered

You lack confidence

You feel insecure

You feel fearful

You are risk-averse

You feel dependent

You feel needy

You feel unprepared

You feel self-loathing

## Key Response

You try to break out from under God's control

# The Passive God

## Key Concept

God is with you, but silent

## His Characteristics

God's there but not present

God is uncaring

God is unable to show affection

God is not interested in family

God is aloof

God never shows Himself

God is stoic

God is silent

God never sticks up for you

## Your Responses

You feel unloved

You feel unprotected

You feel angry

You feel abandoned

You feel unsafe

You feel insecure

## Key Response

You long for someone to care for you

## The Perfectionist God

### Key Concept

God is disappointed

### His Characteristics

God expects 100% perfection

God is demanding

God is unreasonable

God is critical of everything you do

God is never satisfied with your performance

God is never pleased with you

### Your Responses

You feel inadequate

You try harder

You're afraid to make a mistake

You have to do everything perfect

You feel that no matter how hard you try it is never good enough

You feel like a failure if you don't do everything perfect

You are hard on yourself and cannot take a compliment

You always see what you did wrong rather than all you did right

### Key Response

You try to please God through your performance

## The Performance-Oriented God

### Key Concept

God only loves me for what I do

### His Characteristics

God expects peak performance in everything

God only loves and accepts you when you perform

Failure is not an option

God is unrelenting

God is critical of the smallest fault

You can never do or be good enough

2nd place is a loser

God is driven

God is never satisfied

### Your Responses

You feel anxious

You feel pressured

You feel you're not good enough

You are looking for acceptance

You feel unacceptable

You are driven to perform

You are longing to be loved

You feel lacking

You feel tired

You feel like a failure

### Key Response

You either strive to continually perform up to what you believe God's standards are or you grow so tired that you give up.

# Slave Master God

## Key Concept

God is demanding of you

## His Characteristics

God is a cruel taskmaster

God only wants you for what
you can do for Him

God is demanding

God has favorites and you
are not one of them

## Your Responses

You feel used by God

You feel like you are a
piece of property

You feel unappreciated

You feel unnoticed

You feel undervalued

You feel like a second-class
citizen in the kingdom

## Key Response

You feel like you slave away your life
for God and He doesn't even notice
all you do

# The Unapproachable God

## Key Concept

God is absolute perfection

## His Characteristics

God is too holy for you
to approach Him

God is too great to see
the likes of you

God is too busy to have
time for you

## Your Responses

You feel dirty

You feel unworthy

You feel insignificant

You feel unimportant

You feel faraway

You feel separated from God

You feel isolated

## Key Response

You don't even try to approach God
for the fear of being rejected

# Week 1 Day 1

# Examine Your Faith in Christ

Test yourselves to see if you are in the faith;
examine yourselves! Or do you not recognize this
about yourselves, that Jesus Christ is in you—
unless indeed you fail the test?
(2 Corinthians 13:5)

8 For by grace you have been saved through faith;
and that not of yourselves, it is the gift of God;
9 not as a result of works, so that no one may
boast. (Ephesians 2:8-9)

---

**Note:**

The following section *Come to God* is from a blog
post I wrote for the Experiencing His Victory website.
If you would prefer to listen to this in audio format go
to the following link:

experiencinghisvictory.com/45

---

## Come to God

### God Loves You

God loves you with an everlasting love. He wants to have a relationship with
you. God created you out of His desire to be with you.

From before the foundations of the world, God had a plan to make you His son
or daughter. The words that God spoke to the children of Israel hold true for you
today:

11 "For I know the plans I have for you," declares
the Lord, "plans for welfare and not calamity to
give you a future and a hope. 12 Then you will
call upon Me and come and pray to Me, and I will
listen to you. 13 You will seek Me, and find Me,

**when you search for Me with all your heart."**
**(Jeremiah 29:11-13)**

God has great things in store for you, but there is a problem.

## You Are Separated from God

There is only one thing that separates you from God, sin. Romans 3:23 states:

**All have sinned and fallen short of the glory of**
**God.**

You sin when you break any of the commandments of God. When you lie, steal, kill, covet what is not yours, you are choosing to sin.

You sin when you decide to live independent from God and do things your own way and seek to rule your own life apart from God.

You sin when you rebel against God's ways and standards.

## The Consequences of Sin

There are terrible consequences when you sin against God. Listen to the different ways that the Bible describes your condition because of sin in your life.

**Your relationship with God is broken.** Every sin is ultimately against God and it brings a separation in the relationship. You are at enmity with God.

**Because the mind set on the flesh is hostile**
**toward God; for it does not subject itself to the law**
**of God, for it is not even able to do so, and those**
**who are in the flesh cannot please God.**
**(Romans 8:7-8)**

**You die spiritually.** God warned Adam and Eve if they disobeyed Him and ate from the tree of the knowledge of good and evil that they would die. Spiritual death is separation from God. Your spirit dies even though your body and soul are alive.

**16 The Lord God Commanded the man, saying,**
**"From any tree in the garden you may eat freely;**
**17 but from the tree of the knowledge of good and**
**evil you shall not eat, for in the day that you eat**
**from it you will surely die." (Genesis 2:16-17)**

**For the wages of sin is death . . . (Romans 6:23a)**

**And you were dead in your trespasses and sins**
**(Ephesians 2:1)**

16

**You are a slave to sin.** This may seem harsh, but it is true. When you rebel against God you believe you are gaining your freedom. You are not. Instead, you become a slave to sin.

> **Do you not know that when you present**
> **yourselves to someone as slaves for obedience,**
> **you are slaves to the one whom you obey, either**
> **sin resulting in death, or of obedience resulting in**
> **righteousness. (Romans 6:16)**

**You are under the judgment of God.** God knows everything you have ever done in your life and He will hold you responsible for your sin.

> **For all who have sinned without the Law will also**
> **perish without the Law, and all who sinned under**
> **the Law will be judged by the Law; (Romans 2:12)**

> **As it is written**

> **THERE IS NONE RIGHTEOUS, NOT EVEN ONE;**
> **THERE IS NONE WHO UNDERSTANDS, THERE IS**
> **NONE WHO SEEKS FOR GOD; ALL HAVE TURNED**
> **ASIDE, TOGETHER THEY HAVE BECOME**
> **USELESS; THERE IS NONE WHO DOES GOOD,**
> **THERE IS NOT EVEN ONE.**
> **(Romans 3:10-12)**

**You are under the power of the devil.** 1 John 5:19 states that the whole world lies under the power of the evil one. Colossians 1:13 says you are captive in the domain of darkness and in need of rescue by Jesus. Ephesians 2:2 says it is the prince of the power of the air (another name describing the devil) that is at work in the sons of disobedience.

Without Christ you are in a pretty dismal situation. There is nothing you can do through your own efforts that will restore your relationship with God, make you come alive spiritually, set you free from the power of sin, release you from the judgment of God, or get you out of the kingdom of darkness.

I have some good news for you.

## God Has Made a Way

God has a gift for you, Jesus

> **For the wages of sin is death, but the free gift of**
> **God is eternal life in Christ Jesus our Lord.**
> **(Romans 6:23)**

The gift is Jesus and all that He has done for you. It is called salvation through the person of Jesus Christ.

God loves you so much that He provided a way for you to experience life as He intends it to be.

> **For God so loved the world, that He gave His only begotten Son that whoever believes in Him shall not perish, but have eternal life . . . He who believes in Him is not judged; he who does not believe has been judged already, because he has not believed in the name of the only begotten Son of God. (John 3:16, 18)**

## Jesus Shed His Blood for You

God does not want you to remain spiritually dead and separated from Him. God proved His love for you in sending Jesus to make a way back to the Father.

> **But God demonstrates His own love toward us, in that while we were yet sinners, Christ died for us. (Romans 5:8)**

God's plan was for Jesus to be born of a virgin through a miracle of the Holy Spirit so that Jesus could be born spiritually alive and without sin. Jesus then walked in perfect obedience to God all His days without sin. Since He was spotless before God, He could offer His life as a sacrifice for sin allowing you to be cleansed from sin.

> **The next day he [John the Baptist] saw Jesus coming to him and said, "Behold, the Lamb of God who takes away the sin of the world." (John 1:29)**

> **In whom you have redemption through His blood, the forgiveness of our trespasses, according to the riches of His grace. (Ephesians 1:7)**

> **Much more then, having been justified by His blood, we shall be saved from the wrath of God through Him. (Romans 5:9)**

You can now be forgiven for your sins through the shedding of His blood,

But you are still dead and need new life. That is where the resurrection of Jesus comes into play.

## Jesus Rose from the Dead for You

God raised Jesus from the dead because death could not hold Him. Remember it is sin that brings forth death. Jesus died to break the power of sin and rose from the dead to break the power of death.

**But God raised Him up, putting an end to the
agony of death, since it was impossible for Him to
be held in its power. (Act 2:46)**

Since Jesus was raised from the dead we can also rise to new life in Him. The Bible calls this being born again. Jesus told Nicodemus:

**. . . "Truly, truly, I say to you, unless one is born
again he cannot see the kingdom of God.
(John 3:3)**

Peter gives us this insight about being born again:

**Blessed be the God and Father of our Lord Jesus
Christ, who according to His great mercy has
caused us to be born again to a living hope
through the resurrection of Jesus Christ from the
dead. (1 Peter 1:3)**

Look at the wonderful things God did through the resurrection of Jesus from the dead:

- He broke the power of death

- He made life available to you

- You can now be made spiritually alive

- You can be born again

## Jesus is the Only Way

The Bible makes it absolutely clear that salvation comes only through Jesus Christ. There are not many paths to God. All religions are not a way to God. There is only one way to be saved and that is through faith in Jesus Christ.

Jesus made this very clear when He said:

**"I am the way, and the truth, and the life; no one
comes to the Father but through Me." (John 14:6)**

Peter further states:

**And there is salvation in no one else; for there is
no other name under heaven that has been given
among men by which we must be saved.
(Acts 4:12)**

John wrote the following passages:

**But these things have been written so that you may believe that Jesus is the Christ, the Son of God, and that believing you may have life in His name. (John 20:31)**

**But as many as received Him, to them He gave the right to become children of God, even to those who believe in His name. (John 1:12)**

## How to Receive Christ

### Recognize Your Need for a Savior

The first thing you must do is recognize your need for a savior. If you think that you are good enough to save yourself or are trusting in another way to be saved, then you will not come to Jesus.

You must come to Him knowing that you cannot save yourself. You must come to Him recognizing that He is the Savior. He is the way and the truth and the life and that salvation comes through no other name.

### Repent and Turn Toward God

Repentance means having a change of mind resulting in a change of action. The ultimate question is, "Does what you are doing or thinking line up with God's truth?" If not, you must determine to choose God's way, even if what you are doing is socially acceptable. God's word is your ultimate guide.

Repentance means that you accept and come into agreement with what God says. Repentance is, as one author put it, "the 'about-face' of a new commitment." It is where you reject your own thoughts about what is right and wrong and choose to believe what God says is true.

**". . . that they should repent and turn to God, performing deeds appropriate to repentance." (Acts 26:20)**

**"Repent, therefore and return [to God], that your sins might be wiped away, in order that times of refreshing may come from the presence of the Lord." (Acts 3:19)**

### Confess Your Sins

The word confess means to acknowledge. You must come before the Lord and confess your sins, which is agreeing with God that what He calls sin is sin. You agree with God that you have sinned against Him.

**8 If we say we have no sin, we are deceiving ourselves and the truth is not in us. 9 If we confess our sins, He is faithful and righteous to**

20

**forgive us our sins and to cleanse us from all
unrighteousness. 10 If we say that we have not
sinned, we make Him a liar and His word is not in
us. (1 John 1:8-10)**

## Confess Your Faith in Jesus

Once you confess your sins you must also confess your belief that Jesus is the answer for your sin. You are acknowledging your faith that Jesus' death and resurrection frees you from sin and gives you new life. You are receiving the gift of salvation offered through Jesus Christ.

**For by grace you have been saved through faith;
and that not of yourselves, it is a gift from God;
not as a result of works, so that no one may boast.
(Ephesians 2:8-9)**

**9 that if you confess with your mouth Jesus as
Lord, and believe in your heart that God raised
Him from the dead, you will be saved; 10 for with
the heart a person believes, resulting in
righteousness, and with the mouth he confesses,
resulting in salvation. (Romans 10:9-10)**

## Will You Receive Christ?

This is the most important decision you will ever make in your life. It has to do with your eternal destiny. Are you ready to acknowledge your need for Jesus and turn away from your sin and turn to God through faith in Jesus Christ?

If you are ready to make that decision to trust Christ, then I encourage you to turn to God right now and pray. You can go to God and ask Him to forgive you and acknowledge your trust in Christ.

If you would like some help, I have provided a prayer below that will help guide you through the process of coming to God. The words you say are not magical and bring you salvation. It is your faith and trust in Christ that will bring about your salvation.

*Father, I come to you and acknowledge that I am helpless to save myself. I need a savior.*

*I come into agreement with You that I have sinned against you. I have gone my own way and done my own thing. Please forgive me for my sin.*

*I repent and turn away from my sin to come to You. I acknowledge that Jesus Christ is my only hope of salvation. I confess with my mouth that Jesus is my Lord. I believe with my heart that You raised Him from the dead.*

*I receive Your gift of salvation knowing I can do nothing to earn it. I thank you that the blood of Jesus cleanses me from all sin. I thank You that in confessing Christ my spirit is born again and I am at peace with You.*

*Thank you for accepting me. I acknowledge that You are Lord and I give my life to You. Lead me in Your way of life.*

**1. Is there any positive thing in your life you are trusting in for your salvation other than Jesus Christ? (being born into a Christian family, being good, going to church)**

**2. Is there any bad thing in your life that you believe is keeping you from experiencing confidence in your salvation? (I'm too great of a sinner, I've gone too far)**

**3. What do you consider to be the greatest hindrance to your faith?**

**Additional Notes**

**Additional Notes**

# Week 1 Day 2

# Trust in Christ Alone

1 Finally, my brethren, rejoice in the Lord. To write the same things again is no trouble to me, and it is a safeguard for you.

2 Beware of the dogs, beware of the evil workers, beware of the false circumcision; 3 for we are the true circumcision, who worship in the Spirit of God and glory in Christ Jesus and put no confidence in the flesh, 4 although I myself might have confidence even in the flesh. If anyone else has a mind to put confidence in the flesh, I far more: 5 circumcised the eighth day, of the nation of Israel, of the tribe of Benjamin, a Hebrew of Hebrews; as to the Law, a Pharisee; 6 as to zeal, a persecutor of the church; as to the righteousness which is in the Law, found blameless.

7 But whatever things were gain to me, those things I have counted as loss for the sake of Christ. 8 More than that, I count all things to be loss in view of the surpassing value of knowing Christ Jesus my Lord, for whom I have suffered the loss of all things, and count them but rubbish so that I may gain Christ, 9 and may be found in Him, not having a righteousness of my own derived from the Law, but that which is through faith in Christ, the righteousness which comes from God on the basis of faith, 10 that I may know Him and the power of His resurrection and the fellowship of His sufferings, being conformed to His death; 11 in order that I may attain to the resurrection from the dead.

12 Not that I have already obtained it or have already become perfect, but I press on so that I may lay hold of that for which also I was laid hold of by Christ Jesus. 13 Brethren, I do not regard myself as having laid hold of it yet; but one thing I do: forgetting what lies behind and reaching forward to what lies ahead, 14 I press on toward the goal for the prize of the upward call of God in Christ Jesus. 15 Let us therefore, as many as are

**perfect, have this attitude; and if in anything you
have a different attitude, God will reveal that also
to you; 16 however, let us keep living by that same
standard to which we have attained.**

### (Philippians 3:1-16)

Yesterday we looked at the good things and the bad things that get in the way of your salvation. Both the good things and the bad things we do can keep us from coming to Jesus Christ for salvation.

You can either feel too good about yourself and feel no need to come to Jesus or feel so bad that you feel you can't approach God. Either way, you keep yourself from the only one who can save you.

I love this passage by the Apostle Paul. In it, he shows us that even though he had many things he could count on the positive side of the balance scale for salvation, he chose to reject them to receive Christ.

Some think that all Paul was talking about was the good things that he had accomplished, but I think he was talking about more. In verse seven he talks about getting rid of everything that was of gain to him. Then in verse eight he says, "more than that, I count all things to be loss." I believe the "more than that" was all the bad things he did that he regretted from his past.

Good or bad, Paul wasn't going to let anything get in the way of him having Christ and His righteousness.

Your goal today is to purposefully choose to treat like rubbish any good thing or any bad thing that gets in the way of trusting only in the finished work of Jesus Christ for your salvation.

Paul says that he is forgetting everything that lies behind (good and bad) and is reaching forward to what lies ahead. Today is a great day to lay anything aside that does not contribute to your salvation in Christ.

**Choose to count your good things as rubbish**

**1. List any of the things that you answered on question 1 from yesterday. Take a moment and ask the Lord if there are any other things you are trusting in besides Him for salvation and write them down. Once this is complete, repent for trusting in these things, ask the Lord to forgive you, and cast them at His feet as if they were rubbish.**

**Choose to count your bad things as rubbish**

**2. List any of the things that you answered on question 2 from yesterday. Take a moment and ask the Lord if there are any other things that seem to block your assurance of salvation and write them down. Once this is complete, repent for allowing these things to get in the way, ask the Lord to forgive you, and cast them at His feet as if they were rubbish.**

**Additional Notes**

# Week 1 Day 3

# Identify Faulty Views of God

Your view of God affects every single aspect of your relationship with Him. During this week's teaching I spoke of how our earthly fathers many times influence our understanding of God. This is sad, but true.

I then provided you with a list of fourteen faulty views of God, how they make us feel, and the primary way we respond because of it. The various faulty ways we see God are as follows:

- The Absent God
- The Abusive God
- The Angry God
- The Authoritarian God
- The Distant God
- The Good Ole Boy God
- The Indulgent God
- The Legalistic God
- The Overprotective God
- The Passive God
- The Perfectionist God
- The Performance-Orientated God
- The Slave-Master God
- The Unapproachable God

Each one of these views of God will make you respond in different ways in order to win God's favor. They will shape the way you view God and feel about how you think He sees you.

Everyone of the above views is distorted. If you've ever put on someone else's glasses that had a prescription that was way different than your eyesight, you may know what I mean. You put the glasses on and everything changes. Nothing is clear. Everything seems to be totally out of whack. Your stomach begins to churn. You can't see what is really there.

Your goal today is to get as complete of a picture as you possibly can of how you view God. Be as honest as you can. God already knows how you think and feel. It won't surprise Him at all.

Use the views that I provided as a base from which to start. As you answer the questions below put in your own words the way you think and feel. Each of us has our own unique picture of God in our minds and hearts. Just be real and answer the questions to the best of your ability.

**1. Do you relate to any of the faulty views of God presented in this workbook? Which ones?**

**2. List all of the characteristics of God that you believe apply to your view of God and the responses that you feel in your heart.**

**3. Are there any additional things not in the descriptions that you believe about God? Write them down.**

If you are struggling coming up with ungodly beliefs about God, another way is to try and describe how you feel about God or about how you feel He thinks about you.

We can know all the "right" theological things in our minds about God but if our feelings do not match, then we do not really believe what we are thinking in our heads. The problem is that many times we think that a good Christian or a real Christian would not have negative thoughts or feelings about God, so we speak the right things with our mouths while feeling other things in our emotions.

**4. List every feeling that you have about God or the way that he views you. Be as honest as possible. The goal is get these out in the open so you can deal with them.**

**Additional Notes**

# Week 1 Day 4

# The Effects of Your Beliefs

The goal of today's homework is to determine how your faulty views of God affect the way that you respond to Him. For example, if you think that God is angry and waiting for any excuse to punish you, you will not run to Him for help and forgiveness when you sin. You will try and hide from God like Adam and Eve.

Faulty views of God always result in faulty ways of relating to Him. When you run from God, instead of to Him, you cut yourself off from your only source of help. God is the only one who can forgive you. He is the only one who can give you strength to live life as He intends it to be.

Many of the responses you have toward God are at the unconscious level. You instinctively respond to God in accordance to the "gut feeling" of how you believe He looks at you.

The first step to changing a faulty view of God is to put a name to it. You did this yesterday when you listed all your thoughts and feelings about God. The second step is to look at how these thoughts and feelings affect your relationship with God.

Throughout this seminar you are going to learn eight major steps that God uses to bring healing in your life. We are only on step one today. This is the foundational step upon which all the others rely. Your relationship with God is the very source of your life.

Today we will be gathering information we will use later in the course. It's good to remember that healing is a process and God will work on many things during the next weeks and beyond.

Please turn the page and answer the following questions in order to recognize how your view of God impacts your daily life.

**1. Take each of the faulty views of God you wrote down yesterday and describe how each one affects your relationship with God. (I provided an example to get you started)**

| Faulty View of God | Effects on My Life |
|---|---|
| I feel God is harsh and demanding | I try and stay out of His way and live life the best I can |

# Week 1 Day 5

# Repent of All Willful Sin

Every negative thing in your life is caused by sin, either yours or someone else's. I know that it is not politically correct to talk about sin in an age where everyone's first response is, "Don't judge me," but it must be talked about if you want a solution to your problems.

In day one we looked at several Scriptures that spoke about the effects of sin. I want to show you the solution that God has provided for the deadly effects of sin so we can fully participate in it.

> **23 For the wages of sin is death, but the free gift of God is eternal life in Christ Jesus our Lord. (Romans 6:23)**

> **1 And you were dead in your trespasses and sins, 2 in which you formerly walked according to the course of this world, according to the prince of the power of the air, of the spirit that is now working in the sons of disobedience. 3 Among them we too all formerly lived in the lusts of our flesh, indulging the desires of the flesh and of the mind, and were by nature children of wrath, even as the rest. 4 But God, being rich in mercy, because of His great love with which He loved us, 5 even when we were dead in our transgressions, made us alive together with Christ (by grace you have been saved), 6 and raised us up with Him, and seated us with Him in the heavenly places in Christ Jesus, 7 so that in the ages to come He might show the surpassing riches of His grace in kindness toward us in Christ Jesus. 8 For by grace you have been saved through faith; and that not of yourselves, it is the gift of God; 9 not as a result of works, so that no one may boast. 10 For we are His workmanship, created in Christ Jesus for good works, which God prepared beforehand so that we would walk in them. (Ephesians 2:1-10)**

Sin is the most destructive force in the universe. It infests every single aspect of life and if ignored, leads to eternal death. God in His rich mercy sent Jesus to pay the penalty for sin so that you and I could be born again to a living hope and overcome all of the effects of sin in our lives.

Jesus came to save you from sin, heal you from disease, heal your bruised heart, and set you free from demonic influence in your life. He came to give you life and life more abundantly. He died that you might be an overcomer and no longer a slave to sin.

Sin is unbecoming to a believer. It is not a part of who you are in Christ. It goes against the new nature you received from God when you were born again. Jesus died to set you free from the law of sin and death.

It seems that every time I talk about sin there are those who feel a huge weight of condemnation and judgment from God. If you are feeling condemned it is not from God. Recognize the source from where it comes.

It is the devil who is condemning you. He is seeking to paralyze you and keep you in hopelessness and despair. He wants you feeling unworthy and separated from God so that you do not see the hope and freedom that awaits you in Christ.

Many read Romans chapter six as proof that they are judged. They take the negative aspects of the word and hold onto that as truth while neglecting the verses that speak of the promises and possibilities available to the one in Christ.

Years ago I had a friend that every time he talked to me about Scripture it was to prove how wicked and evil he was and how God was judging and condemning him. I was truly amazed at how he could take every negative aspect of a verse and receive it as truth but reject any of the promises of positive things God says about believers.

He, of course, lived a very miserable life. He always focused on the negative aspects of the Gospel and neglected the Good News that in Jesus Christ all of these negative things are taken away.

So I want you to read the following verses with new eyes. Look for the positive things that God is speaking about. Look for the truths about who you are in Christ. Grab hold of the promises God is speaking about and experience the life Jesus died to provide for you.

> **6 What shall we say then? Are we to continue in sin so that grace may increase? 2 May it never be! How shall we who died to sin still live in it? 3 Or do you not know that all of us who have been baptized into Christ Jesus have been baptized into His death? 4 Therefore we have been buried with Him through baptism into death, so that as Christ was raised from the dead through the glory of the Father, so we too might walk in newness of life. 5 For if we have become united with Him in the likeness of His death, certainly we shall also be in the likeness of His resurrection, 6 knowing this, that our old self was crucified with Him, in order that our body of sin might be done away with, so**

that we would no longer be slaves to sin; 7 for he who has died is freed from sin.

8 Now if we have died with Christ, we believe that we shall also live with Him, 9 knowing that Christ, having been raised from the dead, is never to die again; death no longer is master over Him. 10 For the death that He died, He died to sin once for all; but the life that He lives, He lives to God. 11 Even so consider yourselves to be dead to sin, but alive to God in Christ Jesus.

12 Therefore do not let sin reign in your mortal body so that you obey its lusts, 13 and do not go on presenting the members of your body to sin as instruments of unrighteousness; but present yourselves to God as those alive from the dead, and your members as instruments of righteousness to God. 14 For sin shall not be master over you, for you are not under law but under grace.

15 What then? Shall we sin because we are not under law but under grace? May it never be! 16 Do you not know that when you present yourselves to someone as slaves for obedience, you are slaves of the one whom you obey, either of sin resulting in death, or of obedience resulting in righteousness? 17 But thanks be to God that though you were slaves of sin, you became obedient from the heart to that form of teaching to which you were committed, 18 and having been freed from sin, you became slaves of righteousness. 19 I am speaking in human terms because of the weakness of your flesh. For just as you presented your members as slaves to impurity and to lawlessness, resulting in further lawlessness, so now present your members as slaves to righteousness, resulting in sanctification.

20 For when you were slaves of sin, you were free in regard to righteousness. 21 Therefore what benefit were you then deriving from the things of which you are now ashamed? For the outcome of those things is death. 22 But now having been freed from sin and enslaved to God, you derive your benefit, resulting in sanctification, and the outcome, eternal life. 23 For the wages of sin is death, but the free gift of God is eternal life in Christ Jesus our Lord. (Romans 6:1-23)

Pretty powerful stuff. Jesus has done everything you need to walk in victory in Him. This one chapter reveals many truths that if taken to heart will absolutely transform your life. Now that you've read this chapter through I want to give you an assignment. Go to question one and and ask the Lord to help you see all the wonderful truths that He is communicating to you.

**1. Read through Romans 6 again and seek to answer the following questions about each verse realizing that every verse will not have each aspect in it.**

> **What has Christ done for me?**
> **What does it say about me?**
> **What does it say about how I should walk?**

**I will try to help you see what I mean by placing a couple of examples of each question in the following table.**

| What has Christ done for me? | What does it say about me? | What does it say about how I should walk? |
|---|---|---|
| V3 Christ died for me | V2 I have died to sin<br><br>V3 I have been baptized into Christ<br><br>V3 I have been baptized into His death | V1 I should not continue in sin<br><br>V4 I can walk in newness of life. |

| What has Christ done for me? | What does it say about me? | What does it say about how I should walk? |
| --- | --- | --- |
|  |  |  |

I sure hope you enjoyed digging into the truths revealed in this passage of Scripture. It's time to deal with the topic of the day. Are there any areas of your life that you are walking in deliberate sin against the Lord? If so, it's time to make a decision.

It is so easy to let sin creep into your life and just accept it as your norm. It is not helping you grow in Christ. It is causing the very opposite of what you ultimately desire for your life. Sin always brings forth death.

What I want to encourage you to do is to ask the Lord the following questions and respond to His direction. He is Lord of your life and has your best interests at heart. He will never lie to you or lead you astray. He will always lead you into the paths of righteousness for His name's sake.

So take your time and seek the Lord.

**2. Ask the Lord if there is an area of your life that you are willfully sinning against Him? Write down any area the Lord shows you.**

**3. Choose to repent and turn from your sin. Look to God for the power to help you walk in the truths of Romans 6.**

**4. Ask the Lord for insights into what you need to do next to walk in His ways.**

# Week 2

## Ask God for Revelation

### This Week's Goals

- To uncover any ungodly beliefs that are hindering your walk with God and receive God's Truth.

- To recognize any personas that apply to your life and begin the process of change.

- To identify how God speaks to you.

- To commit to believing what God says about you.

- To begin the life-long process of taking every thought captive to the obedience of Christ.

# Week 2 Teaching Notes

**Belief**: a feeling of being sure that . . . something is true.

**Agreement**: a situation in which people share the same opinion: a situation in which people agree.

**Judgment:** the act or process of forming an opinion or making a decision after careful thought: the act of judging something or someone.

**Expectation**: a belief that something will happen or is likely to happen.

**Vow:** a serious promise to do something or act in a certain way.

**Oath**: a solemn usually formal calling upon God to witness to the truth of what one says or to witness that one sincerely intends to do what one says.

## Ungodly Beliefs

All beliefs, agreements, judgments, expectations, vows, and oaths that do not agree with God (His Word, His nature, His character) that cause you to be hopeless and accept your condition as unchangeable

## Ungodly Beliefs

**His Word**: does the thought that you believe line up with God's word? If it doesn't, it needs to be rejected and the truth of God's word received.

**His nature:** does the thought you have line up with who God is in His being?

**His character:** does the thought you have line up with the way God acts? Would Jesus think this way?

**Unchangeable** - The concept here is that things will never change. I am what I am. It is what it is. Nothing can change me or the situation I'm in. Any time you are feeling this way, you are believing an ungodly belief about God, yourself, or others.

## Personas

A Persona is the way that we view ourselves or feel others view us that contradicts the word of God and is based on ungodly beliefs.

A persona is a false image of yourself that is based upon past life-shaping events.

A persona is always based on ungodly beliefs.

A persona always contradicts the word of God.

A persona feels such a part of you that you actually think it is you.

A persona is so much a part of your identity that you feel if you give it up you won't know who you are.

Philippians 1:12-14

2 Timothy 1:8

2 Timothy 1:12

2 Timothy 2:8-10

2 Timothy 4:16-18

## Hearing the Voice of God

John 10:27-28

**God speaks to us through the Bible.**
(2 Tim. 3:16-17)

**God speaks to us through His Son Jesus Christ.**
(Heb. 1:1-3)

**God speaks to us through other people.**

**God speaks to us directly through His still, small voice.**

**God speaks to us by placing a word or short thought into our minds.**

**God speaks to us through a vision.**

**God speaks to us through dreams.**

**God speaks to us through our spirit.**

**God speaks to us through gifts of the Spirit.**
(John 15:14-15)

## Who You are in Christ

A Child of God

A New Creation

A Saint

A Branch

A Sheep

Justified

Dead

A Friend of God

A Person with a
New Heart

A Partaker of God's
Divine Nature

God's Fellow-Worker

An Ambassador

Bought with a Price

Holy

An Overwhelming
Conqueror

God's Own
Possession

## Knowing Who You Are in Christ

# Class Discussion

1. What part of the lesson was most important to you? Why?

2. Describe how ungodly beliefs have negatively affected your life.

3. Which persona do you identify with the most? Why?

4. Describe how God speaks to you and provide an example for the group.

5. Why is it important to learn to hear the voice of God?

6. The Bible tells us to test the spirits to see if they are from God. What tests do you use to determine if a spirit is from God or not?

7. Do you ever read the Bible or hear a sermon and think, "That's not me." or "That's not for me"?

8. Discuss the best way to implement taking every thought captive to the obedience of Christ.

# Personas

| The Orphan | |
|---|---|
| **I Believe** | **I Feel** |
| I'm on my own<br>No one cares about me<br>Whatever I need, I must do it myself<br>I can't count on anyone<br>Everyone has abandoned me<br>I must be strong<br>I can never measure up<br>I will always be alone | Uncared for<br>Unloved<br>Abandoned<br>Deserted<br>Discarded<br>Hardened<br>Lonely<br>Alone<br>Not good enough<br>Isolated<br>Unworthy |

| The Slave | |
|---|---|
| **I Believe** | **I Feel** |
| I'm working my tail off and nobody notices<br>No one appreciates what I do<br>I never get credit for what I do<br>Everyone else gets noticed and recognized except me<br>No one works as hard as I do | Overlooked<br>Neglected<br>Uncared for<br>Jealous<br>Angry<br>Self-pity<br>Joyless<br>Whiney<br>Self-centered<br>Like a martyr |

# The Legalist

| I Believe | I Feel |
|---|---|
| Rules are everything<br>My way is the only right way<br>If you break the rules you're doomed to hell<br>I must make people obey God's word<br>I am the guardian of the truth<br>My anger against sinners is righteous | Contempt<br>Self-righteousness<br>Judgmental<br>Holy<br>Critical<br>Angry<br>Harsh<br>Self-justified<br>Self-appointed judge |

# The Shamed

| I Believe | I Feel |
|---|---|
| I'm bad<br>I'm defective<br>Something is wrong with me<br>I'm damaged<br>I'm dirty<br>I'm unlovable<br>I'm unacceptable<br>If people knew who I really was, they would reject me<br>All compliments I receive are insincere | Small<br>Powerless<br>Unlovable<br>Fearful<br>Embarrassed<br>Ashamed<br>Guilty<br>Dirty<br>Unworthy |

## The Performer

| I Believe | I Feel |
|---|---|
| I must be _____ to be accepted | Lonely |
| No one would ever like the real me | Afraid |
| I can never let my guard down | Unwanted |
| No one cares for the real me | Exhausted |
| I'm a loser | Fake |
| I must always be doing to be accepted | Lacking |
| I have nothing good to offer | Insincere |
| | Needy |

## The Sinner

| I Believe | I Feel |
|---|---|
| I can't help sinning | Evil |
| I'm weak | Dirty |
| I have an evil heart | Depraved |
| I'm only human | Condemned |
| They made me do it | Weak |
| I'm just a sinner saved by grace | Fearful |
| I'm no good | Ashamed |
| There's no hope for me | Unworthy |
| I'm abhorrent to God | Helpless |
| | Hopeless |

# The Codependent

| I Believe | I Feel |
|---|---|
| I must protect and help others<br>My value comes from serving others<br>Other people's needs are more important than mine<br>I must solve other people's problems<br>I must rescue people from themselves<br>If people don't like me it's my fault<br>I must please others to be fulfilled<br>I can't live or survive without (person's name)<br>I can change their behavior<br>I must protect my family at all costs | Responsible<br>Overwhelmed<br>Guilty<br>Ashamed<br>Needy<br>Protective<br>Fearful<br>Indispensable |

# The Independent

| I Believe | I Feel |
|---|---|
| I don't need anyone<br>I'm a self-made man/woman<br>I can do anything better than anyone<br>Needing others means I'm weak<br>Others will just slow me down<br>Others will just let me down<br>I'm better off alone | Rejected<br>Wounded<br>Competitive<br>Superior<br>Fearful<br>Aloof<br>Angry |

# The Impoverished (poverty mindset)

| I Believe | I Feel |
|---|---|
| No matter how much I have, it is never enough<br><br>No matter how much I work, I can never makes ends meet<br><br>I'll never feel secure<br><br>I'll always have to hustle<br><br>I can never relax<br><br>People only like me for what they can get from me<br><br>I can't trust anyone | Lacking<br>Insecure<br>Hopeless<br>Fatalistic<br>Taken advantage of<br>Inferior<br>Insolvent<br>Jealous<br>Envious<br>Angry |

# The Worrier

| I Believe | I Feel |
|---|---|
| I'm a natural, born worrier<br>I have to look out for everyone else<br>I have to be constantly on high alert<br>Someone's got to worry<br>Something bad is going to happen<br>I must keep bad things from happening<br>I must be prepared for every possible situation<br>I'm just protecting myself/my family<br>I only do it because I care | Responsible<br>Over Protective<br>Hyper-alert<br>Anxious<br>Exhausted<br>Impending doom |

# The Bully

| I Believe | I Feel |
|---|---|
| I must prove that I am strong<br>I must intimidate others<br>I must win at all costs<br>I will not let others hurt me<br>I will not let another person control me<br>I must dominate<br>People will respect me or else | Shamed<br>Angry<br>Wounded<br>Inadequate<br>Belittled<br>Alone<br>Isolated<br>Incompetent |

# The People Pleaser

| I Believe | I Feel |
|---|---|
| I must be accepted by everyone<br>I must please people at all costs<br>I must pretend to agree with everyone<br>I can never say no<br>I'm responsible for other people's happiness<br>I feel wanted when people ask me to do things<br>I get my worth through other people | Fearful<br>Unknown<br>Unlovable<br>Lacking<br>Unsafe<br>Needy<br>Unheard<br>Uncared for<br>Unappreciated |

# The Victim

| I Believe | I Feel |
|---|---|
| If something bad happens, it will happen to me<br><br>There's absolutely nothing I can do<br>to change my life<br><br>I'm destined to be used and abused<br><br>It's like there's a sign on my back saying "kick me"<br><br>My life will never change<br><br>No one will ever love me for who I am<br><br>No one will ever protect me<br><br>I can't trust anyone<br><br>People will always abuse me<br><br>I will always get the short end of the stick | Picked on<br><br>Abused<br><br>Targeted<br><br>Defective<br><br>Helpless<br><br>Hopeless<br><br>Powerless<br><br>Defenseless<br><br>Miserable<br><br>Downtrodden<br><br>Limited |

# The Perfectionist

| I Believe | I Feel |
|---|---|
| I must perform well to be accepted<br><br>If I mess up I'm a loser<br><br>If people really knew who I was<br>they would reject me<br><br>Everything I do must be perfect<br><br>No one can do it as good as I can<br><br>It's easier to do it myself<br><br>If it isn't perfect I'm a failure<br><br>If I can't do it perfect, I won't do it at all<br><br>Small goals are not worth pursuing<br><br>Go big or go home | Insecure<br><br>Driven<br><br>Fearful<br><br>Burdened<br><br>Exhausted<br><br>Always having to<br>perform<br><br>Unable to relax<br><br>Longing for recognition |

# Week 2 Day 1

# What is an Ungodly Belief?

## What is an Ungodly Belief?

Today, we want to define the components of an ungodly belief and show the various ways they enter our lives.

## Definition of Ungodly Beliefs

Many authors have definitions for an ungodly belief. One I like comes from Chester and Betsy Kylstra, the founders of Restoring the Foundations. It is a thorough definition and will give me an opportunity to highlight some truths in helping you discern the lies you are believing.

I am thankful for the ministry of Chester and Betsy. Suzette and I have personally received training from them. Their ministry is a blessing to the body of Christ.

Suzette and I have received advanced ministry and completed training through Restoring the Foundations and heartily recommend it for your own personal growth in the Lord.

The Kylstras define ungodly beliefs as:

**All beliefs, decisions, attitudes, agreements, judgments, expectations, vows, and oaths that do not agree with God (His Word, His nature, His character). (emphasis theirs)**

I like the above definition, but I want to alter it a little bit to make an important distinction. My purpose is not to be critical of the Kylstras. I want to show how easy it is to consider actions that flow out of ungodly beliefs as beliefs themselves.

The above definition includes "decisions" and "attitudes" as ungodly beliefs. I do not see them as ungodly beliefs, but as the result of ungodly beliefs. Let's look at each word and see if the focus of the word is on beliefs or results coming from beliefs.

## Decisions

Take the word "decision." A decision is based upon information that is processed in a person's mind. Merriam-Webster dictionary defines a decision as "A choice you make about something after thinking about it: the result of deciding."

The decision is based upon a choice that a person makes from information he or she is contemplating. The ungodly belief is a step below this choice. The three-stage process looks like this:

**Stage 1:** The ungodly belief

**Stage 2:** The process of considering the information

**Stage 3:** The decision made

In case you are wondering, there is a whole process that takes place to form an ungodly belief (we will talk about that later), but since our goal is to define an ungodly belief, we start there for this illustration. So how does this work in a person's life?

**Stage 1.** Bill has an ungodly belief that he is a failure and will never amount to anything. He has believed this most of his life. Bill hates his job. He feels that it is a job that only a loser would do. He constantly talks about getting a better job.

**Stage 2.** Bill's friend Ahmed comes to him one day all excited. He knows Bill hates his job and there is a new opening available in the company. He knows that Bill would be perfect for the job.

Instead of being excited, Bill immediately begins to make excuses why he should not apply for the job. He says, "There are people with more seniority than me. There is no chance in the world I will get the job."

"Are you kidding," said Ahmed, "You are perfect for the job. You have a great chance of getting this job. You've got to apply for it."

"Great," said Bill, "Thanks for the info. I'll think it over."

He did think it over. Fear rose in his heart. He thought, *Why would they choose me when there are better qualified people? Even if I got the job I probably couldn't do it right and they would fire me anyway. I would be out of a job and unable to care for my family. I guess I'm just doomed to remain in this job forever.*

**Stage 3.** As you probably guessed, Bill made the decision to not apply for the job. His decision process was impacted by an ungodly belief that stopped him from having the confidence to try something new.

## Attitudes

Attitudes fall into the same three stages described above. They are a result of making a decision based on beliefs. Let's see how it works in the life of Jana.

**Stage 1.** Jana grew up in a home with a domineering mother. She was never allowed to do things her way. She formed an ungodly belief that everyone was trying to control here life. She made an inner vow that she would never let anyone tell her what to do. She would do it her way.

**Stage 2.** Jana gets a job in a production plant that has specific protocols on how the job is to be completed. After a couple of days, Jana figures out a way she thinks would be better and starts doing it her way.

Her supervisor sees she is not following the protocol. Approaching her, he says, "Jana, you are not following the protocol that I taught you."

"I found a better way to do it."

"Company policy is that we follow protocol. If you feel your way is better, there is a process where you can suggest changes. In the meantime, please follow the protocol."

**Stage 3.** Shaking her head from side, rolling her eyes, and sighing Jana said, "My way is faster and better."

"Still," he said walking away, "I am going to have you do it our way."

Jana's fists tighten and she hit the table. "Why is everyone always trying to tell me what to do? My way is better and he knows it. Who does he think he is anyway?"

Jana looks over her shoulder with a sneer and goes back to doing it her way.

## Focusing on the Fruit Instead of the Root

One of the common mistakes I see people make in their attempt to change things in their lives is that they focus on the fruit rather than the root. They see an action or an attitude that they don't like and try to change it. The problem is that changing the visible things in our lives does not change the invisible.

Let's picture your life as a tree. There are a lot of parts to a tree. We will only be looking at two: the roots and the fruit.

The roots are the invisible part of the tree. They exist and go deep, but are not seen by the naked eye. In this example, the roots are your heart. The fruits are the actions that flow from your heart. These are the outward manifestations that everyone can see. These are the things you try to change.

The roots of a tree provide the nutrients needed to produce fruit. A normal tree only produces one kind of fruit. Your life produces many types of fruit, both good and bad. It is important to see where the source of this fruit comes from.

Jesus tells us it is from the invisible issues of our hearts that the external issues become visible. In explaining a parable to His disciples in Matthew 15:18-20, He shares the following words:

> **But the things that proceed out of the mouth**
> **comes from the heart, and those defile the man.**
> **For out of the heart comes evil thoughts, murders,**
> **adulteries, fornications, thefts, false witness,**

**slanders. These are the things which defile a man .**
. . .

The first word in the list of manifestations Jesus mentions is evil thoughts, what we are calling ungodly beliefs. Ungodly beliefs are the source of all the evil we see in the world. A person thinking godly thoughts would never commit murder, adultery, or any of the other things listed above.

Can you see why it is so important to deal with the root of the issue rather than just the fruit? If you do not take care of the root it will remain to torment you. You will constantly be fighting against the fruit that seeks to pop up out of your heart.

Jesus gives us greater insight into what is taking place in the heart in the Sermon on the Mount. He said:

> **You have heard it was said, 'YOU SHALL NOT COMMIT ADULTERY'; but I say to you that everyone who looks at a woman with lust for her has already committed adultery with her in his heart. (Matthew 5:27-28)**

Jesus is showing us that adultery does not just happen. A person doesn't just walk down the street one day and accidentally or unintentionally commit adultery. The process of adultery begins with thoughts. These thoughts are given place in the heart and move a person toward the actual act of adultery.

As Jesus said, the adultery first takes place in the heart. Therefore if you want to get rid of the fruit of adultery (or any other negative actions), you must deal with the issues of the heart. It is the invisible issues and thoughts of the heart that produce the fruit you do not want.

## Focusing on the Root Instead of the Fruit

Real change comes in your life when you go to the source or the root of the problem, your ungodly beliefs. These beliefs are rarely seen as the source of the problem. Many times you are unaware that you are believing ungodly thoughts until the Lord shows you what they are.

These beliefs are so much a part of your thinking that they are operating on a subconscious level. You have already gone through the thought processes that established the ungodly beliefs and now they are just a part of who you are.

You don't even consciously think about the thoughts. They just flow out of your heart and flavor everything you do.

Let's take a moment to look at the aspects of an ungodly belief to see how they are all based in the realm of thought. They are not the actions that result from the beliefs, but the beliefs themselves. They are the root from which actions flow.

Here is an updated definition of an ungodly belief that leaves out the words "decisions" and "attitudes." It now reads:

**All beliefs, agreements, judgments, expectations, vows, and oaths that do not agree with God (His Word, His nature, His character).**

To get the most out of this definition, let's look at the simple description of each word from Merriam-Webster to see how each is a part of your invisible thought life.

**Belief:** a feeling of being sure that . . . something is true.

> A belief does not have to be true in order to be believed. It just has to feel true. That's why ungodly beliefs are so deadly. They feel like they are true.

> Example: "I feel that God does not love me." We know this is not true because God loves the whole world and sent Christ to die for us.

**Agreement:** a situation in which people share the same opinion: a situation in which people agree.

> An agreement takes place when two people come to the same opinion. This is especially true when dealing with word curses where a person or the devil has spoken something over you and you come to believe it.

> Example: You dad constantly says you are a loser and will never amount to anything. At some point you begin to agree with what is said and personalize it by believing in your heart, "Dad's right, I'm a loser and I'll never amount to anything."

**Judgment:** the act or process of forming an opinion or making a decision after careful thought: the act of judging something or someone.

> A judgment is the end result of thinking about a certain issue. It includes the forming of an opinion of what you believe is true. The judgment can be about God, others, or yourself.

> Example: A person who has been hurt by multiple men might make the judgment, "All men are evil and will hurt me."

**Expectation:** a belief that something will happen or is likely to happen.

> An expectation is a strong belief that something is going to happen. It is generally based on past negative experiences that are projected into the future.

> Example: "Everyone has rejected me in the past. If I make a new relationship, I will also be rejected."

**Vow**: a serious promise to do something or act in a certain way.

> A vow is an inner decision that can be spoken aloud. Its focus is on what a person promises to do or not to do.

Example: The person who was hurt by men might make the inner vow, "I will never let another man hurt me."

**Oath:** a solemn usually formal calling upon God or a god to witness to the truth of what one says or to witness that one sincerely intends to do what one says.

An oath is a vow that someone gives before God. The idea that it is given before God makes it more serious and unchangeable.

Example: "God, I will never let another man hurt me."

**His Word:** does the thought that you believe line up with God's word? If it doesn't, it needs to be rejected and the truth of God's word received.

**His nature:** does the thought you have line up with who God is in His being?

**His character:** does the thought you have line up with the way God acts? Would Jesus think this way?

Now that we have a good understanding of what an ungodly belief is, it is time to ask God to reveal some of the ungodly beliefs you are believing. Go ahead and look through the ungodly beliefs listed below and check each box that relates to your life.

# Possible Ungodly Beliefs

☐ I'm a bad person.

☐ I'm unlovable.

☐ I was a mistake.

☐ I'm ugly.

☐ I'm stupid.

☐ I'm worthless.

☐ I'm a failure.

☐ I'm a sinner. (identity)

☐ I will never amount to anything.

☐ I'm a loser.

☐ I deserve what I get.

☐ I always get the short end of the stick.

☐ If anything bad happens, it will happen to me.

☐ When things go wrong, it's always my fault.

☐ Things will never change.

☐ Things will never get better.

☐ I'm destined to _____.

☐ I'm unimportant.

☐ I'm damaged goods.

☐ Nothing I say matters, so I will just keep my mouth shut.

☐ I'm unlovely.

- [ ] I can't do _____.
- [ ] I'm unwanted.
- [ ] I'm naughty.
- [ ] I'm unfulfilled.
- [ ] I'm irresponsible.
- [ ] I'll never get over _____.
- [ ] I'll never measure up.
- [ ] I'm not worthy of respect.
- [ ] I will never love again.
- [ ] I must put on a mask to be accepted.
- [ ] My marriage is hopeless.
- [ ] I can't do anything right.
- [ ] Everyone would be better off if I were not around.
- [ ] My life is a mistake.
- [ ] Real men don't cry.
- [ ] I'll never be good enough.
- [ ] I must protect myself.
- [ ] I'm a victim.
- [ ] I'm powerless to change.
- [ ] I'm broken beyond repair.
- [ ] I must be perfect.
- [ ] It's somebody else's fault.
- [ ] I will never get credit for what I do.
- [ ] I'm incompetent.
- [ ] God's ways are too restrictive.
- [ ] God is holding back on me.

- [ ] I shouldn't have problems.
- [ ] God has not come through for me.
- [ ] I'm just like my mother/father.
- [ ] I'm dumb.
- [ ] I can't help the way I am.
- [ ] Others have caused my problems.
- [ ] It's my temperament.
- [ ] It's just my personality.
- [ ] it's my upbringing.
- [ ] It's my parents fault.
- [ ] It's my body, I can do with it what I want.
- [ ] I have to stand up for my rights. If I don't do it, who will?
- [ ] I should not have to live with unfulfilled longings.
- [ ] My husband/wife must meet my needs.
- [ ] It's okay to do whatever I need to do to get my "needs" met.
- [ ] The church doesn't need me.
- [ ] I have nothing to offer.
- [ ] God can't forgive me for what I have done.
- [ ] My sins aren't really that bad.
- [ ] I can sin and get away with it.
- [ ] I won't reap what I have sown.
- [ ] I can play with fire and not be burned.

**Add any additional ungodly beliefs on the next page if necessary.**

**Additional Notes**

# Week 2 Day 2

# Identify Your Persona

## Identify Your Persona

Chances are that you are not purely just one persona. There may be a mix of multiple personas that apply to your life. Today's goal is to identify which persona(s) most relate to your life.

**1. Go back to the Week two video's notes and determine which persona most closely describes the way you think and feel about yourself. Write in the area below the most important ones.**

**2. Now list the ungodly beliefs and feelings that you believe and feel and any additional ones not mentioned in the persona chart.**

| My ungodly beliefs | My feelings |
|---|---|
| | |

| My ungodly beliefs | My feelings |
| --- | --- |
| | |

# Week 2 Day 3

# Hearing the Voice of God

Today we want to look at how you personally hear the voice of God.

**1. In the video lesson I described a variety of ways in which God speaks to people. I am listing each way below this question. Write an example of how God has spoken to you in each of these ways. If He hasn't spoken to you in a certain way, don't worry, He hasn't spoken to me in all of them either.**

**God speaks to us through the Bible.**

**God speaks to us through His Son Jesus Christ.**

**God speaks to us through other people.**

**God speaks to us directly through His still, small voice.**

**God speaks to us by placing a word or short thought into our minds.**

**God speaks to us through a vision.**

**God speaks to us through dreams.**

**God speaks to us through our spirit.**

**God speaks to us through the gifts of the Spirit.**

**2. Has God spoken to you in way that is different than any of the ways listed on the previous page? If so, how?**

**3. Take a moment and listen to God. Ask Him if there is anything that He wants to say to you. If He says something, write it down and share it with a friend.**

# Week 2 Day 4

# Knowing Who You Are in Christ

Knowing who you are in Christ is a vital part of growing in the Lord to your full potential. Scripture is full of various pictures and concepts of who you are in Jesus and every one of them is true of you.

The problem is that many times you do not feel what the word says about you and you struggle to walk in that truth. Any time you read something in the Bible and think that's not true of you or that's not for you, you are struggling with an ungodly belief.

The best thing to do is to acknowledge that it is there and then find out why. In order to get rid of ungodly beliefs they must be acknowledged and brought into obedience to Christ. We'll look at that more in day 5.

Today I want you to consider listening to some of the videos I've done on the topic of who you are in Christ. They come from the Experiencing His Victory Academy.

The Academy is the location where all my teaching materials are located in one, simple location. Here is a glimpse of what is inside:

- There are over 700 pages of blog posts compiled by subject for easy reading.
- A video series 24 Forgiveness Myths Busted (in process)
- A video series on Who You Are in Christ (in process)
- A paid course *Healing Your Broken Heart*
- Monthly live training, monthly live Q&A session and access to all paid courses with a paid membership
- For more info go to www.experiencinghisvictory.com/academy

---

**Important Note**
**How to Use the QR Codes on the following pages**

The following pages contain images that you can scan with your iPhone or Google phone which will take you directly to the videos without having to type in any website urls. You must have an app to use them. Here are the apps I suggest you use.

- IOS - QR Code
- Droid - QR Droid

---

# Who You Are in Christ

**1. You Are a Child of God**

**2. You Are a New Creation**

**3. You Are a Saint**

**4. You Are a Branch**

**5. You Are a Sheep**

**6. You Are Justified**

70

**7. You Are Dead**

 **8. You Are a Friend of God**

 **9. You Are a Person with a New Heart**

 **10. You Are a Partaker of God's Divine Nature**

 **11. You Are God's Fellow-Worker**

 **12. You Are God's Ambassador**

 **13. You Are Bought With a Price**

## 14. You Are Holy

## 15. You Are Overwhelmingly a Conqueror

## 16. You Are God's Possession

## 17. You Are God's Witness

If you enjoy these short teachings on who you are in Christ, keep on going back to the Experiencing His Victory website. I am planning on adding many more teachings to this series.

# Week 2 Day 5

# Taking Every Thought Captive

**3 For though we walk in the flesh, we do not war according to the flesh, 4 for the weapons of our warfare are not of the flesh, but divinely powerful for the destruction of fortresses. 5 We are destroying speculations and every lofty thing raised up against the knowledge of God, and we are taking every thought captive to the obedience of Christ, (2 Corinthians 10:3-5)**

The Apostle Paul gives us a clear picture of the weapons that the enemy is using to wage warfare against mankind and the church. His main weapons all are connected to thoughts, ideas, mindsets, and worldviews.

The devil is using words to wage his war. He is using false ideas to hold people in bondage. He is using philosophies and false religions to keep people in captivity.

This should not come as a surprise since Jesus said of the devil that "there is no truth in him. Whenever he speaks a lie he speaks from his own nature, for he is a liar and the father of lies" (John 8:44).

The weapons the devil uses to wage battle are words and ideas. He purposely misleads people with false philosophies and religions to hold them in bondage. We will now look at three ways the enemy promotes his false beliefs.

## Speculations

The first weapon the enemy uses to bring his deceptive viewpoint is through speculations or arguments. The Greek word is *logismos*. There are two important aspects to consider in this word.

The idea behind this word is to bring logic and calculated thought to bear on a topic. It is not just random thoughts thrown at an issue, but a Well-thought-out argument of the rational mind structured to stand against the truth of God's word.

Other words that convey the idea of *logismos* are mindset, philosophy, or worldview. They include both formal and informal arguments that portray the thought process of men on a topic.

The second aspect of *logismos* is the evil intent behind these thoughts. They are opposed to the word of God and seek to contradict what God has revealed. The Louw-Nida Lexicon describes the word as "fallacious and deceptive reasoning and, by implication, based on evil intentions—'false reasoning, false arguments.'"

Dutch Sheets helps us understand the scope of this word in his book *Intercessory Prayer*. He says:

> **These logismos would include philosophies (whether formally identified or unnamed personal ones), religions, humanism, atheism, Hinduism, Buddhism, Islam, racism, intellectualism, . . . materialism, roots of rejection, perversions– anything that causes a person to think a certain way.**

God has revealed Himself through creation, His word, and through Jesus Christ. He has made His truth known and men rise up and contradict it through their own reasonings. They say, "It is not so." Just a few examples should do:

- God says that homosexuality is a sin and an exchange of the "natural function" of a man or woman for that which is "unnatural" (Romans 1:26-27). Proponents of homosexuality argue that this is not true and that it is beautiful when two people are in love with one another.

- God says that the sexual relationship is special and reserved for marriage. Society argues that people should live together and see if they are compatible before they get married.

- God sees abortion as murder. Those in favor of abortion say that it is a woman's right to choose whether or not she should have the baby because it is her body.

- God says through His word that Jesus Christ is the savior of the world and no one can come to Him except through Jesus. There are those that say all religions lead to God and reject the idea that salvation only comes through Jesus.

The list could go on and on as men attempt to contradict what God has called true.

# Every Lofty Thing Raised Up Against the Knowledge of God

Remember that the imagery throughout this passage is one of warfare. The enemy wants to stop the spread of the knowledge of God, so he erects barriers to keep people "protected" from it.

The purpose of these barriers is to keep people from coming to a knowledge of God. It is an active attempt to place a barrier around people that will keep the truth out.

The barriers are erected out of pride. Louw and Nida help us understand the concept behind the word lofty (hypsoma). They describe it as "an exaggerated evaluation of what one is or of what one has done—'conceit, pride, arrogance.'"

74

The resistance and erection of barriers come from a pride that refuses to submit to God. There is a belief that my way is better than God's way. No one can tell me what to do or what is right for me.

Satan rose up in pride and rebelled against God. His plan has not changed from the garden. He arrogantly contradicts the word of God so that people will choose to follow him and not God. He wants men blinded to the truth so he can keep them in his clutches. Second Corinthians 4:3-4 says:

> **And even if our gospel is veiled to those who are perishing, in whose case the god of this world has blinded the minds of the unbelieving so that they may not see the light of the gospel of the glory of Christ, who is the image of God.**

This same attitude is one that Jesus encountered in the lives of the scribes and Pharisees. Jesus warns His disciples of the need of humility since whoever exalts himself will be humbled. He begins to pronounce seven sets of woes against their actions. Two verses are especially meaningful in this context. Jesus said,

> **But woe to you, scribes and Pharisees, hypocrites, because you shut off the kingdom of heaven from people; for you do not enter it yourself, not do you allow those who are entering in to go in. (Matthew 23:13)**

> **Woe to you, scribes and Pharisees, hypocrites, because you travel around on sea and land to make one proselyte; and when he becomes one, you make him twice as much a son of hell as yourselves. (Matthew 23:15)**

The enemy will erect any kind of barrier to stop you from coming to a true knowledge of God.

# Thoughts

The first weapon of the enemy is the big picture reasoning that comprise a philosophy, religion, or a worldview. The second weapon is the barriers he erects to keep people from coming to the truth. The third weapon is specific thoughts directed toward each person.

The Greek word noema has a couple of major ideas. The first is a thought that has come about because of the process of thinking. The second is that of a plan or strategy with evil intents. Have you noticed how the plans of the enemy are based on evil intent?

Paul uses the word to describe the schemes of the devil toward each of us. He says, "we are not ignorant of his schemes" (2 Corinthians 2:11). Part of the war plans of the enemy is specific schemes designed to keep you from the truth.

His plan is unique, though similar, for every person. He knows each person and what makes them tick. He then puts his plan to work by dropping thoughts in a person's mind to keep them in the dark.

C.S. Lewis gets to the heart of this strategy in his book *The Screwtape Letters.* The book is about the correspondence between a senior demon in the "lowerarchy" of hell named Screwtape and his nephew, a Junior Tempter learning how to keep the person to whom he is assigned in the dark and therefore assure his damnation.

Screwtape is constantly telling Wormwood how he should attempt to direct the thinking of his "patient." If the patient begins to respond and move toward God, there is a constant set of directions in how to countermand what is taking place.

Even though this is a fictional book, it gives insight into how the enemy might operate in the life of a human being. The main goal is to keep a person from coming to Christ. If that fails, the next is to keep him passive and irresponsible in the things of God.

The enemy is constantly attempting to speak thoughts to both unbelievers and believers. His goal is to stop them from experiencing a true knowledge of God.

# Erecting Fortresses

Now that we understand the weapons the enemy uses, we can speak about how he uses them to erect fortresses.

The fortresses the enemy is building is not something physical that one can visit and see. It is comprised of the philosophies, religions, worldviews, multiple barriers, and the specific thoughts used to keep people in darkness.

These fortresses are designed to keep men in and God out. There is great power in ideas. What one believes really matters. These fortresses are not a flimsy house of cards that will fall at a slight breeze. They are strongly entrenched ideas that blind the minds of men and women.

It is possible to look at the condition of the world today and despair. But as believers we are not helpless. God has given us weapons to break down the enemy's fortresses.

# Destroying Fortresses

Now we are getting to the fun part. Maybe I am too much of a guy, but I like to destroy things. One of my favorite tools is a Sawzall (reciprocating saw for those with a more refined upbringing). Just give me one those babies and set me loose and I am one happy guy.

The word destroy in the Greek lines up pretty well with the English word destroy. It means to violently pull down, tear down, or demolish. Remember that we are destroying speculations and lofty things exalted above the knowledge of God, not people.

The weapons God gives us are to be used destroy every lie and false precept that does not align itself with the truth of God. We are to tear down stone by stone the walls of lies erected against the truth of God and set people free.

We must also look at our own lives and thoughts and make sure that they align with the truth. If we find anything that is out of line with what God says, we must repent and come into agreement with God.

# Taking Every Thought Captive

When it comes down to it, taking every thought captive is super easy. We just start recognizing the thoughts that are going through our minds and see if they line up with the truth of God's word. We take every lie captive to the obedience of Christ, reject the lie, and counteract it with the truth.

The problem is that we don't always immediately realize that we're thinking wrong thoughts. The ungodly thought is such a part of us we don't see it as a lie. We think it's reality.

If you go through life hearing that you're a loser and believe it with all your heart, soul, and mind, then when you hear that word in your head you won't take it captive. You'll allow it to slip through and continue to negatively affect your life.

A major goal of this week is to begin to think about the process of taking every thought captive and making a life-long commitment to seeking and living by the truth of God's word. That's why we have to bring God and our friends into the picture.

God is the source of all truth and knows the reality of all things. If He says something is true, then it's true. He created you and knows you more intimately than you know yourself. He knows how He has created you and what He has in mind for your life. So, asking for God's help to reveal ungodly beliefs seems like a no brainer.

As we will see in the steps below, asking God to show you every time an ungodly belief flows through you mind is an important part to walking in victory. He knows every thought you think and will show you every time you believe something ungodly, if you ask.

Another way to find out what ungodly beliefs you are believing is to ask your friends to help. Make sure you choose wisely which friends you ask to help. Some friends are not very helpful.

Look for friends who love you and are encouraging. Look for those who are interested in helping you grow in the Lord. Maybe there are only one or two who you can trust to do this. Just ask them to tell you every time you voice an ungodly belief about yourself or others.

Ask them to ask you, "Is that true?" every time they feel you say something they consider to be an ungodly thought. At first this can seem overwhelming and like they are picking on you, but it will force you start looking at the words that come out of your mouth and the thoughts behind the words.

It is also good to recognize that many ungodly thoughts come at times you are thinking about or attempting to do something positive that will help you toward a growth goal. You may have a thought about going back to school and getting a degree in an area of interest. Immediately the ungodly thought rises up, "Why go? You'll never finish. You're just a loser."

The lie stops you in your tracks and you never make the steps necessary to reach your goal. You allow the lie to control your actions. That's why it is important to press through the lie and begin to take steps that counteract the lie.

Instead of outright rejecting going to school, pick up the phone or go online and ask for information about the school you wish to attend. Begin to destroy the ungodly beliefs rejecting them and pressing through the lie and the feelings connected to it.

You are an overcomer in Christ and ungodly beliefs are like chains that bind you. Jesus has broken the chains that have you bound. You must choose to begin to believe what the Lord has done for you start taking steps, even if they are baby steps, toward God's purpose for your life.

All that said, let's look at the steps you can take in taking every thought captive to the obedience of Christ.

## How to Take Every Thought Captive

1.  Determine that you are going to take every thought captive to the obedience of Christ.

2.  Ask God to show you every time an ungodly belief passes through your mind.

3.  Invite friends to question you if they feel you have said something based on an ungodly belief. It can be as simple as asking, "Is that true?"

4.  Once you capture an ungodly belief immediately reject it. Say out loud something like, "No, I'm not a loser." You're voicing your disagreement with the lie. You are rejecting it.

5.  Speak out what the word of God says is true. For example, "I am a child of God and will fulfill His purpose for my life." You may have to look up some Scriptures on the subject to be able to do this part.

6.  Take a step of faith that will counteract the lie and accompanying feelings.

7.  Repeat as often as necessary.

# Week 3

## Take Responsibility for Your Actions

### This Week's Goals

- To recognize that change is only possible by accepting responsibility for your own actions.

- To take full responsibility for your own actions.

- To forgive those who hurt you and release them from the responsibility for your actions.

- To understand the difference between your flesh and demonic influence and how to effectively deal with both.

- To come up with a plan with God to overcome an area of your flesh.

# Week 3 Teaching Notes

**The Blame Game**: It's where we blame someone else for who we are and what we've done.

I blamed my brother for the severe burn on my leg.

I blamed my dad for the way I was. I was an angry person because of his anger.

God said, "You chose to emulate your father."

I chose to be a jerk while resenting my father for being a jerk.

My anger wasn't my dad's fault.

## The Blame Game

# Generational Sin

It's common for children to blame their parents for the choices they make.

It's like an invisible force at work in the family.

**Iniquity**: "to bend", "to twist", or "to deviate from a path."

**Threefold Aspects of Iniquity**

1. The actual sin or wrong behavior

2. The guilt of sin

3. The penalty of that sin

Exodus 34:6-7

Iniquity predisposes us toward the sin.

You're never responsible for your parent's sins.

You cannot blame your parents for your sins.

# Take Responsibility for Your Actions

There's nothing that will keep you stuck in your current condition more than blaming your responses on someone else.

Blaming others locks you into the past with no way forward.

It's so easy to blame others.

Change will never come in your life until you take responsibility for your own actions.

# The Flesh and Demons

"I didn't' recognize that the anger in me was because of a demonic influence in my life.

I thought that the anger was just my flesh.

**The Flesh:** the part of us that refuses to be in submission to God.

Your old man was crucified with Christ.

.

You can't crucify a demon.

You can't cast out the flesh.

You can't blame your sin on the flesh or the devil.

Deut. 30:19

84

# Come Up With a Plan

Find an area of your life that you want to change and go to the Lord and come up with a plan to change it.

I asked the Lord to make flashing red lights appear in my mind.

# Pray With Me

Father, I want to thank You for Your great love for me. Thank You that You love me enough to show me the things that are causing damage in my life. You're not doing it to condemn me. You're doing it to offer me an opportunity of escape through repentance and renunciation.

I ask You to begin to show me things that are my responsibility that I've blamed on others. I want to begin to take responsibility for my choices so that I can change and get my life in order.

Father, forgive me for playing the Blame Game. I make a choice today to stop playing it. I choose to take responsibility for the things I've done. I realize that much of what I blame on others is actually a way for me not to feel responsible for my own sin.

Thank You for Your forgiveness. The blood of Jesus cleanses me from every sin I am willing to confess. Today I choose to turn from the Blame Game to You. Thank you for being there for me. In Jesus' name, Amen.

# Class Discussion

1. What part of the teaching made the greatest impact on your life today?

2. Are you now or have your ever played the blame game? Who were blaming and for what?

2. Discuss the various ways that playing the blame game impacted your life.

3. If you've overcome the blame game, what happened to finally set your free?

4. How has generational sin impacted your family?

5. Will you make a commitment today to give up the blame game and take full responsibility for your actions?

6. Why is it important to know the difference between the influence of the flesh and demonic influence?

# Week 3 Day 1

# Are You Playing the Blame Game?

Are you playing the blame game? Not sure what that is? Then keep on reading.

## Understanding the Blame Game

The blame game is when you blame someone or something in your life for the way you are and the choices you make. It's not your fault that you act a certain way, it's theirs. If they hadn't done this to you, you wouldn't be doing what you are doing.

It's so easy to blame someone else for your actions because it seemingly frees you from personal responsibility. It's their fault I'm the way I am. It's my dad. It's my mom. It's my teacher. It's my boss. It's my husband. It's my wife. It's the economy. It's the government.

The list could go on and on. There are so many people, things, and events to blame for the way you are and the way you act. Here are some possible ways people explain the things they do. See if you can recognize how each statement seeks to justify why they are what they are or did what they did:

- Of course, I'm an angry person, I grew up in a home filled with anger.

- If my wife would have met my needs, I never would have committed adultery.

- When the economy took a nosedive, I had no choice but to start taking money from the company.

- I wouldn't be addicted to drugs if it weren't for Dave. He was the one who pressured me to start taking Meth.

- Why shouldn't I be filled with hatred and bitterness, you don't know what they did to me.

- Me believe in God? Why should I? Christians are just a bunch of hypocrites.

- I can't believe that you shoplifted some clothes. Why do you always do things that make me beat you?

The blame game is always the same. It's always someone or something that is responsible for what you are or what you are doing. If there is any hope of change, it must come through acknowledging the part that you had to play in the situation.

My mother-in-law Kate recently passed away and my wife was able to hear a wonderful story about her mother from one of her nieces. She told about how sometimes she would get in a fight with her husband she would go to Kate's house and tell her all about what her husband had done. Kate would listen patiently to all she had to say and then ask a simple question. "What did you do?"

Kate was very wise and knew that it wasn't just her grandson's actions that needed to be considered. What did you do is a powerful question that forces you to consider the part that you played in the situation.

# David and Bathsheba

I'd like us to consider the story of David and Bathsheba and see how through the process of what took place how David could have excused himself of responsibility for what he was doing and put the blame on others.

David was the king of Israel. It was a time for him to lead his armies in battle, but he decided to send them off to battle and remained in Jerusalem. One evening he got out of bed and went for a walk on the roof of his house and saw a very beautiful woman bathing.

David sent someone to inquire who she was and found out that she was the wife of Uriah, the Hittite. Knowing she was married to one of the soldiers away fighting on the battlefield, he sent for her and had sex with her. She became pregnant.

David came up with a plan to cover his sin with Bathsheba. He called Uriah home off the battlefield so that he would have sexual relations with her and he would think that the child was his.There was only one problem, Uriah refused to go home and be with his wife while his fellow soldiers were on the battlefield.

Uriah chose to sleep at the door of the king's house with his other servants. David called him back and encouraged him to go to his house. Uriah said he could not do such a thing when the ark of the Lord, Joab, the leader of the army, and the rest of his fellow soldiers were sleeping in tents.

David was getting desperate. He called Uriah back again and feed him and kept giving him alcohol until he was drunk hoping this would get him to go home. It did not work, so David sent a message to the leader of the army and told him to put Uriah in the fiercest part of the battle and then pull the army back leaving him alone to die.

Uriah was killed and David thought that he was in the clear. But, of course, he wasn't. God knew what he had done. God sent the prophet Nathan to confront the king with his sin. He had a choice to make would he blame someone else for his deeds or would he take responsibility for his own actions?

Here are some possible things David could have said:

- If Bathsheba hadn't been bathing naked when I was taking my walk on the roof, this never would have happened in the first place.

- If Bathsheba wasn't so beautiful, I'd never have been tempted.

- If she would have resisted my advances, I would never have had sex with her.

- If she had been more careful, she wouldn't have gotten pregnant.

- If only Uriah would have gone to his house, I wouldn't of had to kill him

Nathan the prophet confronted David to his face. David chose to take responsibility for his actions. He told Nathan that he had sinned against the Lord.

# Take Responsibility for Your Actions

It's time to stop the blame game. When you play the blame game it is always someone else's fault. When you blame others you're always the victim and not responsible for your actions. When you blame others you're helpless to change. When you blame others you ensure that things will remain the same.

It's only when you take responsibility for your own actions that things can begin to change. You have absolutely no control over what others do, you only have control over what you choose to do.

I know that terrible things happen to people every day. There are rapes, murders, incest, physical abuse, thefts, slander, betrayals, divorces, and host of other things that cause damage in a person's life.

When these types of things happen, you have a choice to make. You are not helpless. You do not have to remain a victim. You do not have to be permanently shaped by the things that have happened in your life.

There are other options than bitterness, hatred, anger, revenge, fear, worthlessness, guilt, shame, or condemnation. You can choose to make choices that will bring life rather than death.

When I talk like this I always hear in the back of my mind someone saying, sure Terry, you don't know what they did to me. You don't know the pain and heartache I have experienced. You don't have a clue what I've been through. If you did, you would never say what you are saying to me.

Over the past thirty-nine years of being a believer, I have heard many terrible stories of things that people have endured. Terrible things. Things that should never have happened. Horrific things beyond my imagination.

# Two Types of Victims

The English language is wonderful but sometimes we use the same word that has two very different meanings. I recently looked up the word love and it had over twenty meanings. That is why it is important to define the terms that we are using so we can both be on the same page as to what we are talking about.

I want to clarify the use of the word victim. It will help us understand what I am talking about when I say that even though we are a victim we do not have to remain a victim.

The first meaning for victim has to do with something happening to a person from an outside force. You can be a victim of a crime: someone robs you, rapes you, abuses you, tricks you. You are a victim of someone else's sin.

The second meaning of victim has to do with remaining that way for an indefinite period of time. This type of victim believes they deserve what they get. This type of victim says, "My husband left twenty years ago and I'll never be loved by another man. I'm unlovable." A victim mindset says, "I was abused as a child and everyone in my life will always abuse me. I guess it's just my lot in life."

# Two Victims of World War Two

Let's look at the story of two people who were victims of World War II. Both of them saw loved ones killed and experienced terrible things at the hands of the Nazis. One remained a victim for the rest of his life; the other made choices that freed her from being a lifelong victim.

## Yitzhak Zuckerman

Yitzhak Zuckerman was a Polish Jew who was part of the Zionist movement in Poland. He was captured by the Germans brought to a work camp and forced to dig canals and clear swampland.

The conditions were rough. Ten people a day were dying from starvation and being overworked. Others were being shot because the Germans thought they were trying to escape. People would be sitting there talking to you and suddenly die.

The situation was horrific. Yitzhak constantly thought that he was going to die. Before he did he was able to bribe a guard and escape. He became an organizer in the Polish resistance.

The Germans began shipping out 5,000 Jews a day from the Ghetto in Warsaw to Treblinka to be gassed to death. He helped organize the resistance and sought to help people out of the Ghettos through the sewers. The horror of it all had a traumatic effect on his life.

After the war, he began to drink and continued to experience deep mental anguish. He was so filled with bitterness over the events he endured that he told an interviewer, "If you could lick my heart, it would poison you."

## Corrie ten Boom

Corrie lived in Holland when the Nazis invaded in May of 1940. In May of 1942 the family began hiding Jews and members of the Dutch Resistance in their home. An architect came to their home and built a hidden room. It worked well.

On February 28, 1944 a Dutch informant told the Nazis what the ten Booms were doing and they raided their home arresting thirty people. Ten days later her father died. The six people hiding in the secret room were never found and days later escaped to freedom.

After going to trial Corrie, and her older sister, Betsie were sent to Ravensbruck concentration camp. They were treated brutally. Corrie struggled with hating the Nazis, but Betsie always encouraged her to forgive them and put her trust in the Lord.

In December 1944 Betsie died leaving Corrie all alone. But for some strange reason Corrie was released fifteen days later. She learned later that she was released due to a clerical error and that one week after her release they gassed all of the women her age. She had narrowly escaped death at the hands of the Nazis.

One statement that Corrie recalls Betsie making before her death was, "There is no pit so deep that He [God] is not deeper still."

For years after the war, Corrie set up a rehabilitation center to help those who were concentration-camp survivors and for those who were jobless because they collaborated with the Nazis. Then she started speaking about the Lord and her experiences in over sixty nations. During one of her talks she had an experience where she met one of the German soldiers that had been especially cruel.

## Read Corrie's story below

Here is the story in her own words:

When I was in the concentration camp, one of the most terrible things I had to go through was that they stripped us of all our clothes and we had to stand [naked]. The first time was the worst.

I said, "Betsie, I cannot bear this."

And suddenly it was as if I saw Jesus on the cross. And the Bible tells, "They took His garments." He hanged there naked. And I knew He hanged there for me. For my sins. And by my suffering I understood a fraction of the suffering of Jesus Christ and it made me so thankful that I could bear my suffering.

Love so amazing, so divine, demands my life, my soul, my all.

Some people are afraid to look at the cross. Are You? Don't be afraid. The cross is terrible. It's terrible how Jesus suffered. Not to describe, but you must not be afraid to look at it. For if you have been the only person in the world, Jesus would have suffered for your sins.

**At the cross, at the cross**
**Where I first saw the light**
**And the burdens of my soul rolled away.**
**It was there by faith**
**I received my sight**
**And now I have guidance every day.**

It was some time ago that I was in Berlin. And there came a man to me and said,"Ah, Mis ten Boom, I am glad to see you. Don't you know me?"

Suddenly, I saw the man, that was one of the most cruel overseers, guards, in the concentration camp.

And the man said, "I am now a Christian. I found the Lord Jesus. I read my Bible and I know there is forgiveness for all the sins of the whole world. Also for my sins. I have forgiveness for the cruelties I have done. But then, I have asked God's grace for an opportunity that I could ask one of my very victims for forgiveness. Frauline ten Boom, once and you're forgiven. Will you forgive me?

And I could not.

I remember the suffering of my dying sister [Betsie] through him. But when I saw that I could not forgive, suddenly I knew, I myself had no forgiveness. Do you know that Jesus said that? When you do not forgive those who have sinned against you, my Heavenly Father will not forgive you your sins [Mt. 6:15]. And I knew, Oh, I am not ready for Jesus Christ to come real quick for I have no forgiveness for my sins.

And I was not able. I could not. I could only hate him.

And I took one of these beautiful texts, one of these boundless resources, Romans 5:5, "The love of God is shed abroad into our hearts through the Holy Spirit who is given to us."

And I said, "Thank you Jesus that you have brought into my heart God's love through the Holy Spirit who is given to me. And thank you, Father, that Your love is stronger than my hatred and unforgiveness.

That same moment, I was free. I could say, "Brother, give me your hand." And I shook hands with him. And it was as if I felt God's love stream through my arms. You've never touched so the ocean of God's love as that you are forgiving your enemies.

Can you forgive?

No.

92

I can't either.

But He can.

## The Power of Forgiveness to Free

Both stories are powerful. Both stories are possible in your life. The best part of the story is that you have an opportunity to choose life as God intends it to be. You do not have to be a victim your whole life and have a heart filled with bitterness and poison. You can choose God's way.

Both Yitzhak and Corrie were bound in hatred by the tragic events that took place in their lives. One remained a victim even though he was free. The other left victimhood behind as she chose God's way of victory.

Today is the day of God's salvation. Make the choice today to walk in the power of God's love. Reject the role of victim and embrace the life that God has for you today.

**1. Who are you blaming for your sin? List their name and what you are blaming them for. Be thorough.**

**Example**: I blame my dad for making me an angry, violent person.

**2. Look over each of the statements above and honestly answer the question, "Did the person cause me to do what I did or was it my choice in response to their actions? Place a "T" by every statement that is true and an "F" by everyone which is false.**

**Example**: Did my dad cause me to be an angry person? (The answer is False, I chose to respond to his anger with anger)

**3. Are you willing to take responsibility for every statement marked with an "F"? If so, write a statement similar to the example below.**

**Example:** My dad was an angry man and I chose to be an angry person too.

**4. Take time to review every statement you marked with a "T". Are you certain you don't have any personal responsibility for your response to the situation? Be brutal with the truth.**

# Week 3 Day 2

# Understanding Generational Sin

All of us have grown up in some sort of family setting. Some great. Some bad. Some terrible.

## Dealing with Past Family Baggage

There are those who grew up with a mom and dad who were loving and supportive. They were there and helped them through life's difficulties. There were feelings of love, appreciation, and support.

Other grew up with a mom and dad who were caught up in drugs or alcohol. Anger, screaming, violence, and neglect were experienced on a regular basis. There were feelings of fear, insecurity, and abandonment.

There are so many types of families. There are unwed mothers, couples living together with kids, mixed families with children from a variety of moms and dads, grandparents raising kids, foster families, adoptive families, same-sex families to mention a few.

## Traits that Run in the Family

One thing holds true for each of the families mentioned above. Each one has an unseen, invisible atmosphere at work. Even in the best of families there is an invisible force at work to influence it toward evil.

I am sure that you have seen it in other families. There are traits that you can see handed down from generation after generation. Maybe you know a family whose main characteristic is fear. It can be traced from the child, to the mother, to the grandmother, and who knows how many generations in the past.

The characteristics that we are concerned with in this resource are those characteristics that negatively impact family life. They are so much a part of the family that they are considered to be normal. They are so familiar that they are second nature to you. They are a part of how you see yourself, so much so in some cases that you may feel like you are giving up a part of your personality if you were to get rid of them.

A good example of this is a couple of families from my hometown, Austin, MN. I am not going to mention any names, but there were two families that had a reputation for being fighters. All of the guys of the family were fighters. If anyone messed with one of the brothers, you had to face them all.

Or take Bill (not his real name) who grew up in a home filled with sarcasm. Every remark was a smart-aleck response. There was a constant retelling of stories and making fun of one another. Being the youngest boy Bill would continually be harangued by his older brothers.

They always laughed when they said the things they did, so did Bill. He didn't want them to know how deep the words cut into his heart. So, he just went along with the flow. That's just the way his family is.

Bill's heart was deeply wounded. He carried anger, resentment, and bitterness toward his brothers. It is ironic that even though Bill knows how much pain sarcastic words can cause, he didn't realize how deep sarcasm ran in his own life.

## Understanding Iniquity

The Bible calls this invisible influence iniquity. The idea behind this word is "to bend", "to twist", or "to deviate from a path." It is a perversion of what God desires and calls us to be. It is crooked behavior that violates God's commands.

One of the passages in the Bible that shows how iniquity impacts multiple generations is Exodus 34:6-7.

> **Then the LORD passed by in front of him and proclaimed, "The LORD, the LORD God, compassionate and gracious, slow to anger, and abounding in lovingkindness and truth; who keeps lovingkindness for thousands, who forgives iniquity, transgression and sin; yet He will by no means leave the guilty unpunished, visiting the iniquity of fathers on the children and on the grandchildren to the third and fourth generations." (emphasis mine)**

As we see iniquity goes on for three or four generations. It continues to be passed on until something breaks the power of this unseen force. Some people describe the influences of iniquity upon us as generational sin.

## Family Atmosphere

Parents are to be the protectors of the family. When a parent sins in an area of his or her life it opens the door for the enemy to come in and begin to affect the entire family. That is why we see certain characteristics that stick out in generation after generation of a family.

One quick example from the Bible will help us see how this principle works in real life. We are going to examine the role of lying in the lives of Abraham, Isaac, Jacob, and Jacob's sons. These four generations are a snapshot in the lineage of Abraham.

**First Generation**: Abraham. In Genesis 12:10-20 Abram and Sarai went to Egypt because of a terrible famine. Abram was worried that the Pharaoh would kill him because Sarai was so beautiful. He asked her to lie and say that she was his sister.

**Second Generation**: Isaac. In Genesis 26:1-11 we have an almost duplicate situation with Isaac. Another famine took place and he went to Gerar, a Philistine city. He was worried that they would kill him and take Rebekah, his wife. He asked her to lie and say that she was his sister.

**Third Generation:** Jacob and Rebekah. In Genesis 27:11-40, Rebekah encourages Jacob to dress up like his brother to deceive his father and get his brother's blessing. Jacob's mother put goat's hair on her son and dressed him in Esau's clothing to trick Isaac. Jacob is successful and steals his brother's blessing.

**Fourth Generation:** Jacob's ten oldest sons. In Genesis 37:12-36 Joseph is the favored son of his father Jacob. His ten older brothers hate him with a passion. Jacob sends Joseph to check on his brothers to see how they are doing. He travels to Dothan and when his brothers see him they plan on killing him and telling Jacob that he was killed by a wild beast. Reuben, his oldest brother talks them out of killing him, hoping to rescue him later.

In the meanwhile, Joseph's brothers see a Midianite caravan and decide to sell their brother into slavery, that way they would not have to shed innocent blood and make some money on the sale.

They kill a goat and dip Joseph's tunic in the blood and return it to their father. They let him come to the conclusion that his son has been killed. They keep the lie alive for many years.

Lying ran in the family. As you can see it got worse as time passed on. Opening the door to sin will let that influence run rampant in the family lines.

There are many more traits that we can see that travel throughout family lines. This generational iniquity becomes part of the invisible background of the family. It is an unseen force that impacts each person. Many times the person is so used to it that they think nothing of the influence and are blind to it or proud of it.

Here are some further examples of ways that the enemy works in generation after generation through family lines:

- **Competition:** the family is fiercely competitive in everything they do. They want to win and hate to lose. Everyone is always striving to be number one in whatever they do.

- **Fear:** Fear runs through the family. There is constant mention of the bad things that could happen or take place. The first response to any new situation is fear.

- **Pride:** Everyone in the family believes that they are superior to other people. The things they own are better than others, the clothes they wear are the best, and they drive the most expensive cars. They pity those who live normal, boring lives.

- **Guilt**: In this family there is a constant guilt trip. Guilt is used as the foundation of everything. Manipulation is the common way to get anything from the other person.

- **Shame:** People live in a constant silence about the things going on at home. This can be due to drugs, alcohol, or abuse. We can't reveal the things that are happening or it would destroy the family's reputation.

- **Anger:** People in this family have short fuses. Everything seems to irritate them. They are constantly angry and letting everyone know about it. Complaining is natural.

- **Addiction:** Many things continue on in generation after generation. Drug abuse, alcohol abuse, physical or sexual abuse.

One thing needs to be made clear at this point. Because a person lives in this atmosphere does not mean that they are destined to sin in the same way. Sin is always based on a choice you make. No one can make you sin. You do it of your own free will.

What iniquity does is predisposes you toward the sin. It gives you more of an inclination or tendency to respond in the same way as you were raised. More than one author has described it as a pressure that is upon you to sin like your forefathers.

## 1. Think through your family history. What generational sins are evident in your family and how have they influenced you?

# Week 3 Day 3

# Take Responsibility: Forgive

Many people struggle with forgiving those who have hurt them. That's why I want you to remember the story of Corrie ten Boom. She didn't have the strength to forgive on her own, but was able to do so on the spot with the help of the Lord.

What I would like to do is to list twenty-four common reasons people use to not forgive those who have hurt them. Every single one of them is not true when a person has the Lord in their life.

Jesus commands you to be forgiving person, just as He has forgiven you. Forgiveness is a a step of faith and trust in the Lord that He will bring you justice. Forgiveness also frees you from the bitterness and anger and opens up the door for healing to come into your life.

As you read the following myths about forgiveness, place a checkmark beside each one that applies to you. It will make the homework go faster.

I believe that unforgiveness is one of the greatest invisible barriers stopping you from experiencing life as God intends it to be. Freedom will only come as you learn to forgive from the heart.

Unforgiveness binds you to the past. You will never be free unless you learn to be a forgiving person. In trying to help people to freedom, I've noticed that there are many myths about forgiveness that keep people from letting go of unforgiveness.

Open up your heart and receive the truths you are about to hear. It will change your life forever.

## Myth 1 - Forgiving is easy

Sometimes. But more often than not it is hard. The good news is you can choose to forgive, even though the pain.

## Myth 2 - Forgiving gets easier every time you do it

Not really. You can make forgiveness a lifestyle, but that does not ease the pain you feel when wronged.

## Myth 3 - Forgiveness comes with time

Forgiveness is a choice. Time will not cause forgiveness to just happen. It's something that must be acknowledged and released through forgiveness.

## Myth 4 - Some things are too big to forgive

No way. Jesus forgave those who hung Him on the cross and were mocking Him. His blood is enough to cover every sin that is committed on the earth. If Jesus forgives the sins of the world, you can forgive those who have hurt you.

## Myth 5 - Once you forgive that is the end of it

Not always. There may be legal issues to deal with or boundaries that need to be set.

## Myth 6 - Forgiveness is about the other person

Forgiveness is an issue of your heart between you and God. Will you be a forgiving person?

## Myth 7 - Forgiveness means reconciling with the offender

When you forgive, you release the person from your anger, judgment, and thoughts of vengeance. Reconciliation can only take place if the person repents and seeks to restore the relationship.

## Myth 8 - Forgiving is ignoring what happened

In order to forgive something, there needs to be something specific to forgive. You never ignore what took place but face it head on. Forgiveness is acknowledging the wrong and then choosing to forgive the person from the heart.

## Myth 9 - Forgiveness must be earned or deserved

You can forgive without the one who hurt you changing. Forgiveness requires nothing from the person who hurt you or you would be trapped by their unwillingness to change. Forgiveness is a choice of faith that releases the person into the hands of God.

## Myth 10 - Forgiveness is free

Not a chance. Forgiveness is very costly. It costs the one forgiving, but it is well worth the price.

## Myth 11 - Forgiveness is weakness

It takes incredible strength and courage to be a forgiving person. It also takes faith in God and His word.

## Myth 12 - Forgiveness means I will downplay what has happened

You are never to downplay the wrong done against you. You can fully acknowledge the pain you have suffered because of the wrong.

## Myth 13 - Forgiving means forgetting

Can't happen. You will always remember what has happened to you. It will no longer hurt and cause pain. When you forgive you choose not to bring the event up again and use it against a person.

## Myth 14 - Forgiveness can only take place if they ask for forgiveness

Your forgiveness is not dependent upon any response from the one that hurt you. Forgiveness is a choice to forgive as you have been forgiven.

## Myth 15 - Forgiveness means being a doormat

Forgiveness does not mean that you have to allow the person to hurt you over and over again. You can set boundaries and protect yourself from those who hurt you.

## Myth 16 - Forgiveness removes the consequences

When you forgive a person, you release them from your judgment and desires for revenge but not from God's. Vengeance is the Lord's. He will assure that justice is ultimately served.

## Myth 17 - Forgiveness requires me telling the other person they are forgiven

Not necessarily. It is an issue of your heart. If the person repents and asks for forgiveness, you can give it.

## Myth 18 - The person I need to forgive is dead or will not talk with me

Your forgiveness is not dependent on the other person being near. You do not have to have contact with a person to forgive them.

## Myth 19 - I must get over my hurt feelings before I forgive

Forgiveness is not dependent upon being free from pain. Many times healing comes as you forgive. Forgiveness is not based upon your feelings, it is a choice of your will.

## Myth 20 - Forgiveness will instantly heal my wounded heart

This happens much of the time, but not all of the time. Sometimes healing takes time.

## Myth 21 - If I forgive, I will be disloyal to those who were hurt

Forgiveness has to do with loyalty and faith in God. Forgiveness does not mean you agree with what took place, it is a response to the grace of God.

## Myth 22 - Forgiveness means I am letting them off the hook

No way. When you forgive, you are turning that person and the things they have done over to God. You are trusting Him to bring justice to your situation.

## Myth 23 - I can't forgive

Yes, you can. It is a choice of your will. God will help you forgive. Remember Corrie ten Boom.

## Myth 24 - Forgiveness isn't fair

Certainly not from a human perspective. God sees the big picture He will bring justice.

## 1. Write down every myth that you checked as you read leaving enough room to answer the following question. What will you do in order to get beyond the myth and forgive the person(s) who hurt you?

For Example: I can't forgive - Lord, I can't forgive this person in my own strength, Please come to me and help me choose your way. With your help, I choose to be a forgiving person.

**2. List all the people that you blame for causing you to be who you are and for what you've done. Then take responsibility for your actions and pray the follow prayer out loud to ask God to forgive you for blaming them for your actions and release them from responsibility.**

**Example Prayer**: Father, please forgive me for blaming my dad for making me an angry person,. I acknowledge that I chose to be an angry person through my own decisions. I choose to forgive my dad and release him from any responsibility for my choices.

Father, please forgive me for blaming _____ for making me_____, I acknowledge that I chose to be _____ through my own decisions. I choose to forgive_____ and release _____ from any responsibility for my choices.

**Additional Notes**

# Week 3 Day 4
## Understanding the Flesh and the Demonic

There are two major foes that seek to rob you of life as God intends it to be. One is an internal enemy the other is an external enemy that seeks to gain access into your life to steal, kill, and destroy.

The internal enemy is the flesh. It's the sinful nature within you that strives against the work of God in your life. The exterior enemy is Satan and his band of demonic forces. They impact your life through lies, intimidation, and fear.

### The Flesh

The word flesh has multiple meanings in the Scripture, some good and some bad. The good ones speak of our human body which God created. The body is not evil or bad. Even Jesus came in the flesh.

Then there are the bad connotations of the word flesh. They speak of the sinful nature of man that fights against the workings of the Spirit of God through lustful desires and sinful urges. This is not a part of God's creation but the result of the sinfulness of man in his desire to gain something apart from God.

The following Scriptures give us a quick glimpse into the character and results of walking in the flesh:

**5 For those who are according to the flesh set their minds on the things of the flesh, but those who are according to the Spirit, the things of the Spirit. 6 For the mind set on the flesh is death, but the mind set on the Spirit is life and peace,7 because the mind set on the flesh is hostile toward God; for it does not subject itself to the law of God, for it is not even able to do so, 8 and those who are in the flesh cannot please God. (Romans 8:3-8)**

**16 But I say, walk by the Spirit, and you will not carry out the desire of the flesh.17 For the flesh sets its desire against the Spirit, and the Spirit against the flesh; for these are in opposition to one another, so that you may not do the things that you please. 18 But if you are led by the Spirit, you are not under the Law. 19 Now the deeds of the flesh are evident,**

which are: immorality, impurity, sensuality,20 idolatry, sorcery, enmities, strife, jealousy, outbursts of anger, disputes, dissensions, factions, 21 envying, drunkenness, carousing, and things like these, of which I forewarn you, just as I have forewarned you, that those who practice such things will not inherit the kingdom of God. (Galatians 5:16-21)

13 Let no one say when he is tempted, "I am being tempted by God," for God cannot be tempted with evil, and he himself tempts no one. 14 But each person is tempted when he is lured and enticed by his own desire. 15 Then desire when it has conceived gives birth to sin, and sin when it is fully grown brings forth death. (James 1:13-15)

15 Do not love the world or the things in the world. If anyone loves the world, the love of the Father is not in him. 16 For all that is in the world—the desires of the flesh and the desires of the eyes and pride of life—is not from the Father but is from the world. 17 And the world is passing away along with its desires, but whoever does the will of God abides forever. (1 John 2:15-17)

As you can see from the above passages, there is nothing good at all in the flesh. It's opposed to God and fights against Him in every possible way. It is the fleshly desires inside of you urging you to do what is wrong. The end result is always death.

## The Flesh Must Be Crucified

The Bible says that there is only one thing to do with the flesh. Kill it! Here are a few of the verses that speak about how we are to treat the flesh every time it raises its ugly head in us.

24 Then Jesus told his disciples, "If anyone would come after me, let him deny himself and take up his cross and follow me. (Matthew 16:24)

6 We know that our old self was crucified with him in order that the body of sin might be brought to nothing, so that we would no longer be enslaved to sin. 7 For one who has died has been set free from sin. (Roman 6:6-7)

**24 Now those who belong to Christ Jesus**
**have crucified the flesh with its passions**
**and desires. (Galatians 5:24)**

**5 Put to death therefore what is earthly in you:**
**sexual immorality, impurity, passion, evil desire,**
**and covetousness, which is idolatry.**
**(Colossians 3:5)**

There is only one cure for the flesh. It must die. You must make a conscious choice to reject the cravings within you and place them on the cross. You are not expected to do this in your own strength. You're to do it in the power of the Holy Spirit.

Your flesh is weak and unable to stand against the power of the flesh. Jesus came to destroy the works of the devil and release you from the power of your flesh. This is accomplished by recognizing that you are crucified with Christ and Christ lives in you and empowers you to walk victorious through the power of the Holy Spirit.

You must deny yourself. You must crucify your flesh. You must put to death the passions that are drawing you away from God with the help of the Holy Spirit.

## Demonic Powers

The Scripture is also clear that we have an array of demonic forces that are seeking our destruction. They have schemes and designs to rob you of the life that God has for you.

**10 Finally, be strong in the Lord and in the**
**strength of his might. 11 Put on the whole armor**
**of God, that you may be able to stand against the**
**schemes of the devil. 12 For we do not wrestle**
**against flesh and blood, but against the rulers,**
**against the authorities, against the cosmic**
**powers over this present darkness, against the**
**spiritual forces of evil in the heavenly places.**
**13 Therefore take up the whole armor of God, that**
**you may be able to withstand in the evil day, and**
**having done all, to stand firm.**
**(Ephesians 6:10-13)**

**11 so that we would not be outwitted by Satan;**
**for we are not ignorant of his designs.**
**(2 Corinthians 2:11)**

**8 Be sober-minded; be watchful. Your adversary**
**the devil prowls around like a roaring lion,**
**seeking someone to devour. 9 Resist him, firm in**
**your faith, knowing that the same kinds of**

**suffering are being experienced by your
brotherhood throughout the world. (1 Peter 5:8-9)**

You don't have to be afraid of the devil, but you don't want to be flippant either. The word of God tells you to be sober-minded, watchful, to put on the whole armor of God so you can stand victorious against all of these strategies.

## Demons Must Be Cast Out

You can't be nice to demons. You must learn to stand in the authority of Christ and command them to leave your life. Just remember that you cannot crucify a demon. I tried that for years with the anger I had. You must cast them out.

We'll be talking about your authority over all the works of the devil in the retreat. I will leave that teaching until then. At the retreat you will gain insight into how you can resist the devil and force Him to leave your life. Wahoo!

The goal of today's teaching is to make you aware of the difference between the flesh and the devil and how they must be treated differently if you are to defeat them and enter into the fulness God has for your life.

**1.  Go back through this teaching, especially the Scriptures, and list all of the negative things the Bible speaks about the flesh. Seek to understand how these desires work in your life.**

**2. Go back through the teaching, this time look for God's answer to overcoming the flesh and think of some ways you could put the truths you learned into practice in your life.**

**3. Look at the passages of Scripture under the heading Demonic Powers and make some observations about your enemy. What are his goals for your life? What are his tactics? Consider how he has worked in your life.**

**Additional Notes**

# Week 3 Day 5

# Come Up with a Plan

Today's goal is to take one area of your life that concerns you and come up with plan for change with the Lord.

## Getting Out of the Rut

Let me be clear, sometimes when God reveals the truth everything changes, habits and all. But sometimes we are so programmed in responding a certain way that it takes a conscious effort for us to put off the old and put on the new. The Apostle Paul says:

> **22 that, in reference to your former manner of life, you lay aside the old self, which is being corrupted in accordance with the lusts of deceit, 23 and that you be renewed in the spirit of your mind, 24 and put on the new self, which in the likeness of God has been created in righteousness and holiness of the truth. (Ephesians 4:22-24)**

When you were held by an ungodly belief you learned to operate out of the lies. You patterned your life and responses from those lies. Your responses become instant and automatic. You have responded in a way so many times it takes no conscious thought. You do it automatically.

How many times have you experienced this truth in your own life? A situation takes place and you respond negatively. Instantly there is deep regret because you do not want to act that way. It just happens without any thought.

This is a learned response that has become ingrained in your actions. You have responded from the lie so many times it has become second nature. You just respond.

That was true for me when I first came to the Lord. My problem was with anger. I would instantly respond to certain situations with anger and arguing. I hated it and wanted it to stop.

No matter how many times I told myself, "I will not get angry or argue," I responded with anger and argued to win. Finally, in desperation, I cried out to the Lord.

I told the Lord that anger just flew out of me before I really had a chance to stop it. I felt helpless. I asked the Lord if He would help me and give me an opportunity to respond before I blew up and acted in a way I hated.

To make sure I had a chance to respond I asked the Lord to set off a flashing red light in my mind as a reminder that I had a choice to make.

One day shortly after that, the Operations Officer in my squadron came to me and began to chew me out for something one of my troops did wrong. I sucked in a deep breath and raised my hand ready to argue with him.

I saw the red flashing light in my mind.

I put my hand down, lowered my head, and said, "I'm sorry, sir."

He said, "That's okay," and left.

I was shocked. It worked. I could stop the anger that always rose up in my heart. I could react differently than I always did before. Wahoo!

I always love it when the Lord begins to show me how I can live differently in Him. I don't have to stay the same, think the same, or react the same. I can make a choice to agree with what God says is true.

Paul shows you a three-step process you can go through to see these changes come to play in your life. He said:

1.    Lay aside your old self (corrupted in accordance with the lust of deceit)

2.    Be renewed in the spirit of your mind

3.    Put on the new self (in the likeness of God)

## Putting Off the Old Self

The first stage of the process is laying aside the old self. This means laying aside all of our old beliefs and actions that do not line up with God's truth. Before you came to Christ, you did not have the power to do this. But now you do.

The power of the Holy Spirit in you gives you the ability to put off the old man. Taking off the old man deals with the casting off ungodly beliefs and ungodly actions.

Paul talks about it as a former way of life. Now that you have come to Christ you can put off the way you used to live and put on what God has for you.

The former ways are corrupt. They are worn out, useless, and deceitful. They did not produce life, only death and destruction.

The way to put this off is by accepting and walking in the truth. Paul tells you to be renewed in your mind. We have seen throughout this seminar that ungodly beliefs hold you in captivity and keep you from experiencing the life of God.

It is the renewing of your mind that allows you to make choices leading to life. Your thoughts and mind must come into agreement with the truth of God's word. You must allow Him to shape our understanding of life and godliness.

The only way to be free from an ungodly belief is to recognize it as a lie and embrace the truth of God's word. When you allow God's word to shape your thoughts, you can renounce the lie and have your thinking changed. Changed thinking results in the possibility of a changed life.

Understanding the truth in your mind is not enough. You must put the truth into practice. It is never enough to reject the lie and accept the truth. You must repent and renounce the lies.

True repentance is agreeing with God's truth and thereby begin to walk in it. True repentance leads to a true change in your thoughts and actions. You are never to just get rid of the old. You must also put on the new.

Getting rid of something is only a partial victory. God calls us to get rid of the old but has something incredible to replace it.

## Putting on the New Self

These new clothes are not something we provide for ourselves. They are already provided and they are in the likeness of God and created in righteousness and truth.

The Apostle Peter puts it this way:

> **His divine power has granted to us all things that
> pertain to life and godliness, through the
> knowledge of Him who called us to His own glory
> and excellence, by which He promised to us his
> precious and very great promises, so that through
> them you may become partakers of the divine
> nature, having escaped from the corruption that is
> in the world because of sinful desire.**
> **(2 Peter 1:3-5)**

God gives you the power and ability to escape the corruption that comes through sinful desires and put on the new man, which is actually partaking in His divine nature. When you reject the old way of life, accept the truth of God's word, you are able to put on the new man and walk in newness of life by the power of the Holy Spirit.

It is God's divine power that has made all of these things available. It is much like the weapons of your warfare that are divinely powerful. God has provided what you need to live a fruitful, overcoming life.

The Christian life is not a life of self-effort. Too many are trying to live the Christian life in the power of the flesh through rules and regulations rather than by the power of the Holy Spirit. This will always lead to defeat and hopelessness.

God does not want you to struggle in your own strength and abilities. God has provided whatever you need to live a godly life. It is already a finished work and available to you through faith.

Paul tells you to make the choice to reject and put off the things in the past that are corrupt and bring death into your life. He invites you to have your mind renewed so that you can come into agreement with the truth of God's word. Once you know the truth you must grab hold of the new self made available through the power of God.

God has given you everything you need for life and godliness. It is when you embrace His truth with faith and walk not in your own strength but His that you live life as God intends it to be.

An important thing to remember is that all that you need is already available and waiting for you to put on. It is not something that God needs to do. He has already done it. It is waiting for you.

## Take Responsibility

Often, you ask God to do things that you are supposed to do. You pray, "God take this from me, while God is asking us to take it off. Or we ask God to give us something that He has already given, while He is waiting for us to put it on.

God will not do what He requires you to do in response to Him. It is your responsibility to put off and put on, not God's. It is your responsibility to walk by faith. No one else can do it for us.

It's time for you go to the Lord and make a plan to overcome the things of the flesh that are getting in the way of your growth in Christ. Answering the questions below will be a step in the right direction.

**1. Choose an area of the flesh you want to see changed in your life. If you are struggling to come up with something or there are so many things in your life to overcome and you are not sure where to start, ask the Lord. Write down the area you want to change.**

**2. Think through the negative consequences of the action in your life and the benefits of getting rid of it.**

Consequences                              Benefits

**3. Pray through the situation and come up with a plan with the Lord's help on how you can begin to change this area of your life.**

**4. Come up with a plan if you fail to complete the plan. What will you do if you fail?**

**Example:** When I made my plan with God, it didn't go perfectly. It was a process. So, the plan was that if I got angry with a person, I would either immediately or as soon as possible apologize, say "I'm sorry for being angry that's is not the type of person I want to be," and ask for their forgiveness.

**5. Put your plan in to action.**

# Week 4

## Repent and Renounce

## This Week's Goals

- To understand the true nature of repentance.

- To understand the true nature of renunciation.

- To repent of and renounce your faulty views of God, ungodly beliefs, your personas, and generational sins.

# Week 4 Teaching Notes

Repentance is the catalyst of change in your life.

Repentance is more than feeling sorry.

Repentance is more than changing your mind.

Repentance is more than apologizing.

Romans 7:14-25

Feeling bad about what you have done and agreeing with God that it was wrong is only partial repentance.

Esau - Gen. 27:32-38

Hebrews 12:15-17

## Repent and Turn to God

## Esau: False Repentance

# The Prodigal Son - True Repentance

**Definition:** Though in English a focal component of repent is the sorrow or contrition that a person experiences because of sin, the emphasis in μετανοέω and μετάνοια seems to be more specifically the total change, both in thought and behavior, with respect to how one should both think and act.

Prodigal son
Luke 15:11-32

He came to his senses.

He Returned to his father.

He confessed his sin.

He changed his actions.

Acts 3:19

Acts 20:21

No change in lifestyle. No Repentance.

## Renounce and Turn from Sin

**Definition:** To renounce is to make a formal declaration that you refuse to follow, obey, or recognize any longer the things you once did or held as truth. When you renounce, you're telling the devil and everyone who will listen that you want nothing more to do with this in your life.

2 Corinthians 4:2

2 Corinthians 2:11

Ephesians 4:27

1 Peter 5:8

Ephesians 6:12

James 4:7

Mark 3:27

Luke 10:19-20

What's the opposite of God? Nothing!

Renouncing always turns a back on sin.

Renouncing breaks things in the spiritual dimension.

Father, strengthen me with Your power to stand on the truth of Your word and repent for anything that I've done that You consider to be sin. Help me take responsibility for what I've done and to come to you to receive forgiveness and cleansing. I chose to follow Your ways.

And Satan, I chose today to break every agreement that I've ever made with you. I renounce the deeds of darkness that I have participated in and choose to align myself with God and His ways. I no longer submit myself to you or your ways. I am choosing today to follow God.

In Jesus' name. Amen

# Class Discussion

1. What part of the teaching made the greatest impact on your life today?

2. What are the key similarities and differences between Esau's repentance and the prodigal sons?

3. What do you see as the defining characteristic of true repentance?

4. Discuss the concept of renunciation and any possibly ways to apply it to your life.

5. Renouncing is to be done out loud and directed toward the devil. On a scale of 1 to 10, how high is your confidence in doing this? Why?

6. Terry mentioned there is nothing opposite of God. What are some of the major differences between God and the devil? Why are these differences important to note?

# Week 4 Day 1

# Understanding True Repentance

What comes to mind when I say the word repent? Do you see some wild-eyed prophet pacing the street with a sign in his hand in all capital letters declaring REPENT! THE END IS NEAR? Do you feel judged and condemned wishing that those critical, judgmental Christians would just shut up and leave you alone? Or do you see it, like I do, as one of the greatest gifts God gives you to know His truth and come to Him?

## An Incomplete Understanding of Repentance

One of the dangers I see in American Christianity is that we've equated belief and faith in Jesus Christ with a list of doctrinal beliefs. We believe that simply because we've been taught something, and we know it intellectually that we actually believe it.

That's the problem my dad had with Christians. Every time I tried to talk to him about coming to Christ, he would go on a tirade about the hypocrites who went out on Saturday night, got drunk, and then went to church on Sunday.

It was hard for my dad to believe that the people he was talking about really had a relationship with Jesus when they lived like the devil all week and then went to church on Sunday. He knew deep down in his gut that if they are true followers of Christ, they would not be acting that way on a continuous basis.

In the same way, I see there is also a misunderstanding of true Biblical repentance. For many, the concept of repentance doesn't go far enough. Here are the main ones I see.

## I'm Sorry

Some equate repentance with feeling bad about what they've done, apologizing, and promising never to do it again. This, of course, is wonderful but it doesn't go far enough.

It reminds me of a commercial I saw years ago. A man is sitting at the kitchen table. He is drunk and holding his head in his hands. You can see that he is filled with remorse.

He says, "I'm so sorry, it'll never happen again."

The video stops and begins to rewind. You see the picture moving back to the beginning and hear the words going backward at a fast, high pitch. He then says the same words, "I'm sorry. It'll never happen again." I don't remember how many times it rewinds, but as it rewinds a person comes on talking about the need to break the cycle of addiction.

The problem with feeling bad is that it doesn't change the situation. There is more to repentance than saying I'm sorry.

## Changing Your Mind

Part of the meaning the word repent is to change your mind. This is the most common understanding that people have about repentance. It is changing one's mind and agreeing with what God says.

This is one hundred percent true, but it doesn't go far enough. It doesn't change the situation. It reminds me of the Apostle Paul and the struggle that He had in dealing with sin in his life. He tells us in Romans 7:14-25:

> **4 For we know that the Law is spiritual, but I am of flesh, sold into bondage to sin. 15 For what I am doing, I do not understand; for I am not practicing what I would like to do, but I am doing the very thing I hate. 16 But if I do the very thing I do not want to do, I agree with the Law, confessing that the Law is good. 17 So now, no longer am I the one doing it, but sin which dwells in me. 18 For I know that nothing good dwells in me, that is, in my flesh; for the willing is present in me, but the doing of the good is not. 19 For the good that I want, I do not do, but I practice the very evil that I do not want. 20 But if I am doing the very thing I do not want, I am no longer the one doing it, but sin which dwells in me.**
>
> **21 I find then the principle that evil is present in me, the one who wants to do good. 22 For I joyfully concur with the law of God in the inner man, 23 but I see a different law in the members of my body, waging war against the law of my mind and making me a prisoner of the law of sin which is in my members. 24 Wretched man that I am! Who will set me free from the body of this death? 25 Thanks be to God through Jesus Christ our Lord! So then, on the one hand I myself with my mind am serving the law of God, but on the other, with my flesh the law of sin.**

Paul is showing us how he's in total agreement with what God says. He knows the things he is doing are wrong, he doesn't want to do them. and he even hates doing them. He wants to do good, his heart is in the right place, but he is not changing and feels totally helpless wondering who will set him free from this hopeless situation.

So, we see that feeling bad about what you are doing and agreeing with God that what you are doing is wrong is only partial repentance. For true repentance to take place there must also be a change of action. Jesus gave the perfect example of true repentance in one His parables.

## An Example of True Repentance

Jesus enters the temple and the chief priests and the elders of the people confront Him and ask who gave Him authority to do the things that He's doing. Rather than answering them, he asks them whether the baptism of John was from God or from men. Instant dilemma.

They know if they say from heaven, then Jesus was going to ask them why they haven't repented and believed. If they say from man, they were afraid of the people because they believed he was a prophet. So, they refuse to answer.

Jesus gives a simple parable that shows true repentance and rebukes them for their unbelief. He said:

> **28 "But what do you think? A man had two sons, and he came to the first and said, 'Son, go work today in the vineyard.' 29 And he answered, 'I will not'; but afterward he regretted it and went. 30 The man came to the second and said the same thing; and he answered, 'I will, sir'; but he did not go. 31 Which of the two did the will of his father?" They \*said, "The first." Jesus \*said to them, "Truly I say to you that the tax collectors and prostitutes will get into the kingdom of God before you. 32 For John came to you in the way of righteousness and you did not believe him; but the tax collectors and prostitutes did believe him; and you, seeing this, did not even feel remorse afterward so as to believe him.**

So, let's compare the four groups of people and find out what Jesus believed to be true repentance:

- The first son refused - felt bad - changed his mind - went to the field

- The second son agreed - didn't feel bad - changed his mind - didn't go to the field

- The tax collectors and prostitutes sinned - felt bad - changed their minds - believed

- The chief priests and rulers didn't feel bad - did not change their minds - refused to believe.

An important side note is an understanding of the word believe. Belief in the Bible is not a mere mental assent, but always carries the idea of actions that flow from that belief. For example, the tax collectors believed the message of John and were baptized by him. True belief requires putting something into practice.

There are three components of repentance: regret, a change of mind, and a change of action. Let's focus on the last component of action. True repentance always has an element of turning away from something and turning to something else.

# Turning From . . . Turning To

I always like to get my understanding of truth from the word of God. It's the only firm foundation for life and doing things God's way always releases His blessing on our lives.

One of the main words for repent in Old Testament Hebrew is šûb. The New Bible Dictionary, Third Edition explains the meaning of šûb as "the call for repentance on the part of man is a call for him to return (šûb) to his creaturely covenant and dependence on God."

The article goes on to say that the:

> **NT usage is much more influenced by the OT šûb; that is, repentance not just a feeling sorry, or changing one's mind, but as a turning round, a complete alteration of the basic motivation and direction of one's life. This is why the best translation for metanoeo is often 'to convert', that is, 'to turn round'.**

In Acts 3:19 Peter tells his listeners:

> **Therefore, repent and return, so that your sins may be wiped away, in order that times of refreshing may come from the presence of the Lord.**

Paul proclaims the same concept when speaking to the elders of the church at Ephesus. He said he was "solemnly testifying to both Jews and Greeks of repentance toward God and faith in the Lord Jesus Christ." (Acts 20:21)

It is so clear that Biblical repentance requires not only sorrow for sin, but a change of mind, followed by a change in lifestyle. No change in lifestyle, no repentance.

> **Therefore, leaving the elementary teaching about the Christ, let us press on to maturity, not laying again the foundation of repentance from dead works and of faith toward God. (Hebrews 6:1)**

For Paul repentance from dead works and faith in God go hand in hand. You must turn from one to the other. Repentance will change not only the things that you think but also the things that you do.

So in order to wrap this up, I want to leave us with my favorite definition of repentance I have found so far. It is by Louw and Nida, two Greek experts. They say:

**Though in English a focal component of repent is the sorrow or contrition that a person experiences because of sin, the emphasis in μετανοέω and μετάνοια seems to be more specifically the total change, both in thought and behavior, with respect to how one should both think and act.**

True repentance requires a change in action. The way to know if you truly believe is by your actions.

Thank You, God, for leading us in the pathway of repentance. Show us any place where we need to change not only our thoughts, but also our actions.

## 1. In your own words write the definition of true repentance.

## 2. Do you have an example from your life where you truly repented. If so, what were the results?

**3. True repentance has multiple aspects to it. Read through the article and write down what you think the main components of repentance are.**

**4. Looking at the components of true repentance that you listed above, explain why each one is important and why all of them together are absolutely necessary.**

# Week 4 Day 2
# Renunciation: Putting the Devil on Notice

Have you ever talked to the devil? No, I don't mean carry on a conversation like you're good friends. I mean, have you ever stood up to the devil and told him no more. Have you ever told him that you will not believe His lies or follow his ways any longer? If you haven't, maybe it's time you did.

## The Need to Renounce

I believe there is a part of the healing process that is often overlooked called renouncing. Once God shows you a lie you've been believing and you repent and receive God's truth, it's time to renounce. You boldly tell the devil that you reject his lies and will have nothing to do with them from that point on.

The Apostle Paul wrote:

> **but we have renounced the things hidden because of shame, not walking in craftiness or adulterating the word of God, but by the manifestation of truth commending ourselves to every man's conscience in the sight of God.
> (2 Corinthians 4:2)**

The concept in the Greek language is to disown, renounce, forbid, reject. The idea is that you were doing or believing something and now you no longer do it or believe it.

To renounce is to make a formal declaration that you refuse to follow, obey, or recognize any longer the things you once did or held as truth. When you renounce, you are telling the devil and everyone who will listen that you want nothing more to do with this in your life.

## Be Alert for the Devil

Some people get nervous when I start talking about the devil. They say things like, "Aren't you paying too much attention to the devil? If you told God you're sorry and changed your mind, why bring the devil into the situation?"

The main reason I talk about the devil is because the Bible does. There are dozens and dozens of passages that speak about the devil and his work. The word of God says the following about the devil:

- You are not to be ignorant of his schemes (2 Corinthians 2:11)

- You are warned not to give the devil a foothold (Ephesians 4:27)

- You are to be of sober spirit and be on the alert because the devil is prowling around like a lion seeking whom he may devour (1 Peter 5:8)

- You do not fight against flesh and blood but against the rulers, against the powers, against the world forces of this darkness, and against spiritual forces of wickedness in the heavenly places. (Ephesians 6:12)

- You are to submit to God and resist the devil and he will flee for us. (James 4:7)

- Jesus talks about binding the strongman (Mark 3:27)

- Jesus gives you authority over all the works of the enemy (Luke 10:19)

There are many more verses that speak of the nature and character of the devil. The good news is that Jesus has given you power over the enemy. If you are ignorant you can fall into the trap of the enemy, but the Bible teaches you his ways so that you will not fall into his traps.

# God is Greater Than the Devil

Just so we get this straight, let me tell you that the devil is a created being and is minuscule in comparison to God. Jesus said that if I cast out demons by the finger of God, then the kingdom of God is at hand. (Luke 11:20)

Did you catch that Jesus is casting the demons out by the finger of God? It is like us flicking a bug off our arm. It takes hardly any effort at all.

I'm leading a pastor's conference way out in the sticks in Mozambique. I am asking the pastors a series of questions. I am not trying to trick them, I just want to see what they'll say.

So I ask them to tell what is the opposite of words I am about to say.

I say, "What is the opposite of up?"

They say, "Down."

"What is the opposite of hot?"

"Cold."

"What is the opposite of high?"

"Low."

Then here comes the biggie, "What is the opposite of God?"

They all said, "The devil."

130

"No, no, no, no, no," I said. There's nothing opposite of God.

There is only one God and no one in all of creation is like Him. He is one of kind. Nothing even comes close. Everything apart from God is created. He is the uncreated one. Everything else has limitations. He is the limitless one.

So then, if the devil is so weak in comparison to God, then why even bring him up. Because the Bible does. He can deceive us, lie to us, scare us, tempt us, intimidate us, but beyond that he is lacking in power. We're to be on the alert for the devil is prowling, resist him, and stand strong in the truth of the Lord.

## Put the Devil on Notice

I said all of that to say why we must stand up to the devil and renounce anything to do with him or his lies. If we have willingly participated in his lies, we must willingly stand up and renounce anything to do with them.

Renouncing is declaring that we will have nothing to do with these lies or lifestyle any longer. Where we have willingly participated in sin, we stand up and say, "No more! I'm drawing a line in the sand and I will not cross it."

## How does Renouncing fit into the Eight Steps to Experiencing His Victory?

In step one you examine your relationship with God to make sure that you know Him and that you are not in any way sinning against Him.

In step two you ask God for revelation. You asked Him to show you if there was any harmful way in you. You can be deceived, but God cannot. He is faithful to show you the areas of your life that need to be changed.

Step three is to take responsibility for your actions. If you have sinned against God, you must acknowledge that or you will make no progress. You must be like David who said he sinned against God and no one else.

Step four is to repent. Repentance is always toward God. You agree with what He says and turn to Him.

Step five is renouncing. You have already come into agreement with God over your sin, now you must stand up to the devil and renounce your former ways. Renouncing always turns a back on sin. It is no longer a part of your life.

So when you put steps four and five together you can say that you formally accept what God says is true and formally renounce the lies you once held. Repentance is toward God. Renouncing is toward the devil. Renouncing is putting the devil on notice.

A great thing about public renouncing is that there are others who bear witness to what you are saying. God hears it, the devil hears it, and all who are present hear it. Most of all, you hear it.

When you verbally renounce the things of the devil, there is a breaking in the spiritual dimension. Things change when you declare you will no longer walk in agreement with the devil.

I'm thinking. Is there anything that you need to renounce? If so, put the devil on notice.

## 1. In your own words write a definition for the word renounce.

## 2. Look through some of the Scriptures in today's reading and describe what your relationship with the devil is supposed to be like.

**Example:** I shouldn't be ignorant of his schemes. He is out to harm me.

# Week 4 Day 3

# Putting it into Practice 1

Today you are going to put into practice the truths you learned about repenting and renouncing. You will retrieve information from earlier lessons to help you through this process.

## Dealing with Faulty Views of Salvation

The following questions deal with any of the good things or bad things you wrote down for questions 1 and 2 for the homework for Week 1 Day 2. You already repented for these beliefs. The reason I have this series of questions is if you are still struggling with any of the issues. If you are, we will walk through them one by one. If you are not struggling in this are, then you can skip to question 4.

**1. Look back on your answers to questions 1 and 2 from Week 1 Day 2 to see if you are still struggling with any of the things listed. If you are, write down the items below.**

| Good Things (question 1) | Bad Things (question 2) |
|---|---|
| | |

**2. Choose to repent from trusting in any of the good things listed in question 1 and put your faith completely on what Christ has done on your behalf.**

**Example:** Father, I repent for trusting in being baptized as a baby for my salvation. I renounce my belief in that lie and choose to put my faith in you alone. Please forgive me and cleanse me from any influence this lie has had upon my life. In Jesus' name.

Go back to your list in question 1 and say the following prayer out loud for each item.

> **Father, I repent for trusting in _____ for my salvation. I renounce my belief in that lie and choose to put my faith in you alone. Please forgive me and cleanse me from any influence this lie has had upon my life. In Jesus' name.**

**3. Choose to repent of any bad things listed in question 1 that you allowed to get in the way of fully trusting in Christ for salvation.**

**Example:** Father, I repent for believing that I was so bad You could never truly forgive me. I renounce that lie and freely receive Your forgiveness for what I have done. I choose today to believe that the blood of Jesus Christ cleanses me from all sin and draws me to Your side.

Go back to your list in question 1 and say the following prayer out loud for each item.

> **Father, I repent for believing that_____. I renounce that lie and freely receive Your forgiveness for what I have done. I choose today to believe that the blood of Jesus Christ cleanses me from all sin and draws me to Your side.**

134

**4. List any faulty views of God that you wrote in questions 1-4 on Week 1 Day 3, then move on to question 5.**

| My Faulty View of God | The Truth God Revealed |
|---|---|
| Example: God is a slave driver | Example: God is my loving Father |
| | |

Read question five before using this prayer

**Father, I repent for believing that You _____ and I renounce the lie. Please forgive me and reveal to me who you truly are.**

(Now listen to see what He says)

**5. Choose to repent and renounce every faulty view of God that you listed in question 4 above. Use the prayer at the bottom of the previous page to deal with each lie one by one. See the instructions below.**

Now that you have every faulty view of God listed in the question above. It is time to repent and renounce each one. This will help break the power of the lie and get you ready for the next step of the process.

You have been believing a lie about God. Now it is time to seek God for His truth. After repenting and renouncing, you will take time to hear from God.

Go through the following steps for each ungodly belief you listed in question 4.

1. Take one faulty view of God at a time and say the prayer listed at the bottom of question 4. (See the example below in question 5)

2. Once you've repented and renounced the faulty view, take a moment to ask the Lord what truth He would like to revel to you about Himself concerning the lie. Write down His truth in the column opposite of the faulty belief so you can meditate on it later.

3. Continue the process until you have gone through every faulty view listed in question 4.

Example: Father, I repent for believing that you are a slave driver only expecting me to serve you as your slave. I renounce this lie and ask you to forgive me for believing it. Open my eyes to the truth of who you are.

# Week 4 Day 4

# Putting it into Practice 2

Today's goal is to gather together every ungodly belief you listed in week 2 and work through them one at a time and receive a word from the Lord in response to that lie.

I know this may seem overwhelming, especially if you have a lot of ungodly beliefs listed. Don't be overwhelmed. Go through as many as you can today and if there are any remaining you can come back to this page later and continue to work through the process.

Getting free from ungodly beliefs is a continuous process and there is no need to press through every ungodly belief today.  It can be quite emotionally exhausting to go through the process.

The main thing is to learn and understand how to go through this process so that you can use it for the rest of your life any time you discover you are believing an ungodly belief.

**1. Use this and the following page to write list your ungodly beliefs and the truths the Lord shows you. The prayer to walk through is at the bottom of the following page.**

| My Ungodly Beliefs | Truth God Reveals |
| --- | --- |
|  |  |

| My Ungodly Beliefs | Truth God Reveals |
|---|---|
|  |  |

Father, I repent for receiving and believing the ungodly belief that
_____.  I renounce it as a lie and will not give it place in my life any
longer. I ask you to forgive me and cleanse me of its effects on my life. I choose
to forgive anyone who played a part in my believing this lie. I forgive (say who
they are and how they did this) _____ for _____. I also choose to
forgive myself for believing it. I ask you now to reveal to me the truth that You
have for me concerning this lie. I receive the truth that _____ (write what
the Lord tells you opposite the lie on the previous page)

138

# Week 4 Day 5

# Putting it into Practice 3

Today you are going to break off the influence of past generations. On Day 2 of Week 3 you listed any of the sinful patterns that you see in your family lines. We are now going to break the influence of the iniquity off of your life and release the blessing of the Lord in its place.

**1. Go to the homework from Week 3 Day 2 and list all of the generational sins you came up with in the area below. Then using the prayer at the bottom of the page go through each item one at a time.**

I acknowledge the sin of _____ in the generational lines of my family. I repent for any place that I have participated in that sin. I renounce _____ and want nothing to do with it any longer. I break the power of this sin in my life and command every demonic force connected with it to leave my life now.

I choose to forgive and release my ancestors for their involvement in this sin and the effect it has had on my life. I ask that You would release your blessing in my life and give me the strength to walk in Your fulness.

# Week 5

## Let Jesus Restore Your Soul

## This Week's Goals

- To become aware of the ways that pain effects your life.

- To understand the place emotions play in your life and that God experiences many of the same emotions.

- To help expose the various coping mechanisms you use to help yourself deal with the pain.

- To understand that Jesus knows the pain you are experiencing because He experienced it Himself and bore it for you on the cross.

- To provide insights into how to get the most out of your retreat experience.

# Week 5 Teaching Notes

**Let Jesus Restore Your Soul**

Colossians 1:13-14

2 Peter 1:3-4

Ephesians 1:3

Isaiah 53:1-10

## Jesus Experienced Great Pain

Betrayal

Abandonment

Denial

Injustice

Slander

Rejection

Physical Abuse

Mockery

The Weight of Sin

Forsaken by God

The Wrath of God

Psalm 22:1-18

**Jesus Paid to Heal Your Pain**

Psalm 34:18

Psalm 147:3

Psalm 23:2

Isaiah 61:1-3

Isaiah 61:7

# Coping Mechanisms

Ignore the Pain

Stuff the Pain

Accept the Pain

Rehearse the Pain

Medicate the Pain

Emulate the Pain

## God's Plan to Heal Your Pain

1. Invite Jesus into your process

2. Ask Jesus which situation He wants to Heal

3. Forgive those who hurt you

4. Give Jesus your pain

5. Ask Jesus to heal your broken heart

6. Break any demonic influence

7. Receive God's blessings

# Class Discussion

1. What part of the teaching made the greatest impact on your life today?

2. Discuss the various ways that Jesus knows your pain.

3. On a scale of 1 to 10, how confident are you that Jesus can heal your pain? Why?

4. Terry spoke about six coping mechanisms we use to try and deal with pain. Can you relate to any of them? They are:

> Ignore it
> Stuff it
> Accept it
> Rehearse it
> Medicate it
> Emulate it

5. Many people struggle to forgive those who have hurt them. Are there things you struggle with in the area of forgiveness? What do you struggle with? Why?

# Week 5 Day 1

# How Wounds Effect Us

## Woundedness

We live in a broken world deeply impacted by the power of sin. Man's rebellion against God has brought chaos and destruction into the world that has touched the life of every person on the planet.

Talk to anyone around you and if you talk long enough you will hear a story that caused that person pain. Each of us carry wounds deep in our souls that effect the way we view the world around us.

The wounds that you carry are invisible barriers to spiritual growth. These wounds hinder you from being everything God created you to be. Many go about life not realizing the impact wounds from the past have in their lives.

## How Wounds Effect Us

I am sure that I don't need to tell you the various ways pain can enter your life. I'm sure, if you wanted to, you could give me a long list of the wounds you have received over the years. The exact details of how we were wounded may vary, but the pain that impacts us is similar.

I want to list some of the various types of events that can cause brokenness in our lives and then talk about how these wounds can effect us. For example:

- You are five years old, your mom and dad argue, he walks out the door never to return.

- Your best friend betrays you and tells your deepest, darkest secret to all who will listen.

- You grow up in a home with an abusive alcoholic parent.

- You are sexually abused or raped.

- You are constantly made fun of by those around you. You are the focal point for every joke.

- You put everything you had into a business adventure and it failed.

- Your mom said, "I wish you were never born."

- Your husband leaves you for another woman. Your wife leaves you for another man.

- Someone is spreading vicious, ugly rumors about you that others believe to be true.

- A drunk driver causes an accident that kills one or more family members.

The list could go on and on, but you get the point. There are so many events in our lives that can cause us pain and heartache. Let's look at an example of how these tragic events cause pain and influence our lives.

## Laura's Story

[This story is told through the eyes of an adult looking back on events in the past. It represents many of the stories I have heard over years of ministry]

Hi, I'm Laura, I am five years old. I love playing in my room with my dolls. I love to mother them and care for their every need. We were having a tea party. As I start pouring tea for my guests, I hear my father start screaming in the other room.

Immediately fear grips my heart and mind. My stomach tightens up. I begin to shake. I want everything to go well between mom and dad. Tears start flowing down my cheeks.

I want the arguing to stop, but it doesn't. Their voices just keep getting louder and louder.

I cover my ears with my hands to block out the arguing. "Please stop. Please stop," I say over and over.

Even though I know what is coming, my body jerks when I hear the sharp crack of my father slapping my mother and the dull thud of her body hitting the floor.

I run into the living room and see my mother lying on the floor weeping. My father is standing over her shaking with rage. I see a suitcase by the door.

I say, "Don't hit mommy any more daddy. I'll be good,"

He turns to me in rage. He is so angry that I almost pass out. He screams at me, "Get back in your room now,"

I know that look, so filled with hatred and disgust. As I turn to leave the room he turns, grabs his suitcase, and storms out the door.

I never see him again, but he still haunts me. I will never forget the look in his eyes the day he left.

150

## Laura's Pain

Some form of Laura's story is experienced every day. The events may change, but the results are the same. A little girl filled with pain because of the choice someone else makes.

So many of the things that effect our lives are caused by the people we love. Laura's dad should have loved her and protected her. Instead he was abusive and walked out of her life. These kind of actions cause a lot of heartache in a little girl's life.

Heartache is a good word to describe the way we are feeling. These events cause pain that we carry around with us. Some have described this pain with words like, "It felt like he stabbed me in the heart."

Emotional pain is every bit as real as physical pain. It hurts. It hurts bad.

So let's look at some of ways pain entered Laura's heart.

## Through Abandonment

God's plan for the family is to be a place of safety and nurture. Her father was to be her protector and provider. His love was to provide a sense of worth, security, and confidence in Laura. But that all changed the day he walked out the door.

Laura's first feelings were fear. "Where is he going?" "When will he come back?" Then her mom told her he would not be coming back. Pain entered her heart as she thought, "If my dad loved me, he would never have left."

She felt the insecurity of being abandoned. She felt unloved and uncared for. She cried a lot and started clinging to her mother like glue. She wondered if she was going to leave her too.

## Through Guilt and Self-Condemnation

Laura thought through the days before her father left. She remember that he had yelled at her quite a bit during that time. He would say things like, "You're such a brat. You'll never learn to listen." "I don't know why we ever decided to have kids. Life would be so much easier without you."

It was then that Laura understood (incorrectly) that it was her fault that her dad left. If only she would have been better and listened and been obedient, her dad would not have left. She took all the responsibility for her father's actions and another level of pain entered her heart.

Not only did she have to deal with her father being gone, but it was all her fault that he left.

## Through Rejection

It did not take her long to come to the conclusion that the reason her father could not love her was because she was unlovable. No matter how hard she had tired, her father left.

Then she started thinking about some of the fights she had with her friend. She remember the words she said, "You're not my friend any more. I don't like you anymore. Suzie, is my friend now."

The more she thought about it the more she knew that she was unlovable. No one could ever love her and her pain deepened.

## Through Self-Hatred

Knowing she was unlovable, Laura turned more and more inward. She started looking at every part of her life trying to determine why she was so unlovely.

She remembered the words her father had said, "You're such a brat. You'll never learn to listen." I can never do anything right, she thought. What's wrong with me? Why can't I do things the right way?

In addition, she had thought, If I was only as beautiful as Suzie or smart like Jonie, then I would be lovable. The more she looked at herself the less she liked herself. It was all her fault nobody loved her. She was defective.

She began to loathe who she was. The pain deepened further still.

## 1. List some of the key events in your life that have caused you pain.

## 2. What are the key emotions these events raised in your life?

Example: Laura felt fear, rejected, guilty, and abandoned.

## 3. How have these events caused you to respond to yourself?

Example: Laura felt self-condemnation felling she was the reason her father left and self-hatred because of the many ways she was unlovable.

## 4. How have these events caused you to respond to other people?

Example: Laura became very clingy to her mother and withdrawn from others to escape being hurt again.

# Week 5 Day 2

# The Problem with Pain

## The Problem with Pain

The main problem with pain is that it hurts. We don't like the pain and the negative feelings that are associated with pain. So we try to get rid of pain as quickly as we can.

Part of the pain we experience when bad things happen to us include a variety of emotional responses. These include anger, sorrow, grief, depression, bitterness, and hatred.

People deal with pain in a variety of ways, which we will look at shortly, but before we do we should look at some reasons why God would want us to experience pain and negative emotions.

## Many Think Negative Emotions are Bad or Evil

Many believers are out of touch with their feelings. They actually believe that the emotions they are experiencing are bad and evil. If they were a "good" Christian they would not have to deal with depression, anger, sadness, hatred, or grief.

Any time they experience a strong emotion they immediately turn away from it, thinking that it is evil or of the flesh. If it feels bad it must be bad. This thinking is incorrect and gets in the way of a person's emotional health.

The reason I say that strong emotions in themselves are not evil is because God Himself experiences strong emotions and He is holy and emotionally whole. If these emotions are evil, then God would have nothing to do with them. God experiencing them shows us the validity of the emotions.

The Bible shows us that God the Father, Jesus the Son, and the Holy Spirit all experience what we consider to be negative emotions. Let's look at how each of the members of the Trinity experienced strong emotions.

## God Experiences Anger

> **"Now again the anger of the LORD burned against Israel . . ." (2 Samuel 24:1).**

The phrase "anger of the Lord" is used 35 times in the Bible to describe God's response to the sinfulness of man. God experiences anger. God's anger burns against injustice, idolatry, the shedding of innocent blood, taking advantage of the poor, the weak, children, and widows.

Anger is a strong emotion. So much so that many people want to get rid of it as something evil. God's anger burned. It was strong and it was pointed at unrighteousness.

Some things should make us angry. When a grown man beats a little baby because it does not stop crying. When a mother drowns her children because she no longer wants to care for them. Or when someone scams an eighty-year-old woman out her life savings. We should be angry.

The Bible does deal with the idea of anger and what we should do with it.

**"BE ANGRY, AND yet DO NOT SIN; do not let the
sun go down on your anger, and do not give the
devil an opportunity" (Ephesians 4:26-27).**

Anger is not the problem. What we do with anger is. The Bible tells us to deal with our anger quickly and not allow it to fester. When anger festers it builds into unforgiveness, rage, bitterness, craving for revenge, and other undesirable feelings and emotions that give place to the devil.

We can see what takes place when anger is given an opportunity to simmer. There are times when the anger erupts and brings its destructive effects with it. Racial unrest erupts into riots that cause millions of dollars damage and further anger.

One group holds anger and hatred toward the other. They seek some way of revenge and cause great harm. The group that was hurt is stirred to more anger and hatred and seeks revenge. The cycle continues endlessly every day across our world.

The devil will take every opportunity to stir up anger, division, and strife. He loves it when you hold anger in your heart. It gives him an opportunity to bring his destruction into your life.

Learn to use anger the right way. Anger is a signal that something is wrong. When you are angry take a moment to stop and find out why. It is there for a reason and many times not the reason we think.

We say, "You made me so angry." Many times it is not the person that made you angry. You were responding to something else. That is where investigating why the anger is there and dealing with the real issue is so important.

When you take time to ask God why you are angry, He will show you. When He does, you will be able to start dealing with the real source of your anger.

Some of the causes of anger are past hurts, guilt over something we have done or not done, feelings of injustice, or feeling overwhelmed. Once you determine why you are angry you can bring the issue to the Lord and and walk through the process of healing.

## The Holy Spirit Experiences Grief

**"And do not grieve the Holy Spirit of God, by whom you were sealed for the day of redemption." (Ephesians 4:30)**

There are many verses in the Bible about the Holy Spirit. As far as I know there is only one strong negative emotion attributed to the Holy Spirit: grief. I am sure that there are many things that cause the Spirit to be grieved.

The Spirit can be blasphemed (Matthew 12:31). No, blasphemy is not swearing or cursing. It means to slander or to speak lightly of sacred things. The Jewish leaders were convinced that Jesus cast out demons by the power of the devil. It was the Holy Spirit's power doing this. They slandered the work of the Holy Spirit by saying the source was demonic.

The Spirit can also be insulted (Hebrews 10:29). The idea is of a person considering oneself to be superior and insults through their disdain for a person or thing.

The Spirit experiences grief when the church lives in disarray. In Ephesians chapter four Paul's encouragement of not grieving the Spirit is surrounded by words like stealing, unwholesome words, bitterness, wrath, clamor, slander, and malice.

When the church acts this way the Holy Spirit experiences emotional pain. The idea of grief is a sadness caused by the pain one experiences in their soul. This pain resulted from the ungodly actions of members of the church in Ephesus. The Spirit saw what they were doing and was grieved.

## Jesus Experienced Deep Emotional Pain

**"And He took with Him Peter, and James, and John, and began to be very distressed and troubled. And He said to them, 'My soul is deeply grieved to the point of death: remain here and keep watch." (Mark 14:32-33)**

**"And being in agony He was praying very fervently; and His sweat became like drops of blood, falling down upon the ground."
(Luke 22:44)**

It is in the Garden of Gethsemane that we see the humanness of Jesus most clearly. For months He was telling His disciples that He was going to go to Jerusalem, be rejected by the leaders there, and be beaten, crucified, and resurrected after three days.

Jesus knew the time of His betrayal and His death on the cross had come. He knew He was going to face rejection, beatings, scourging, and the painful death of crucifixion. The weight of what was coming came crashing down on Him as He entered the garden.

The Gospels use some powerful words to describe the emotions that Jesus felt. There is no way for me to adequately describe what took place in the heart and mind Jesus. There is no way for you to understand the struggle and depth of emotion that Jesus went through that night.

Let's look at the meanings of some of the words used to describe the almost overwhelming emotions Jesus dealt with His final night before the crucifixion. Jesus became **"very distressed."** The idea behind this word is that Jesus was greatly amazed, astonished, alarmed. The full emotional impact of what He was facing hit Him all of the sudden.

Powerful emotions rose up in Him. He was **"grieved"** (sorrowful and distressed) and **"distressed"** (be full of heaviness, be very heavy." He wasn't just grieved, he was **"deeply grieved"** (exceedingly sorrowful, extremely afflicted, profoundly sorrowful).

The emotions Jesus was feeling were so strong and impacting that Jesus told Peter, James, and John that His soul was **"deeply grieved to the point of death."** Jesus was feeling the full weight of what was coming. He had a choice to make and so He prayed to the Father.

Jesus was in **"agony."** This word describes a struggle taking place in Jesus for victory. An inner battle raged as Jesus fervently prayed that what was about to happen would not  happen. The internal battle was so strong that Jesus sweat drops of blood.

He asked God three times if there was any other way. Three times He knew there was not. Three times He told God that His will be done, not His own. He won the battle over His emotions and willingly went to the cross.

You are an emotional being, but you don't have be driven or overcome by emotions. There is no need to run from your emotions or try not to experience them. God created you in His image. Emotions are part of the package.

Jesus is an example that no matter how strong the emotions, they can be dealt with if you bring them to the Lord in prayer. When Jesus was faced with His agonizing decision, He took it to the Father. It was in prayer that He won the victory.

1. What is your attitude toward emotions? Do you see them as something good that God has given you to know what is going on in side of you? Or, do you see them as bad things to be avoided at all cost? Do your best to describe how you view your emotions.

2. Today's reading described the strong emotions experienced by God. The Father's anger, the Spirit's Grief, and Jesus' deep emotional pain. How does knowing that God experiences these emotions help or hinder your dealing with the emotions you experiencing in life?

**3. In the last part of the article we talked about how Jesus had powerful, overwhelming emotions, yet He still chose to be obedient to the Father. Write down some of the emotions you deal with and how you react to them positively or negatively.**

# Week 5 Day 3

# How We Deal with Pain

## How We Deal with Pain

As you can see, much of the pain that you experience comes through the events that take place in your life and the thoughts you have surrounding the events.

Every person deals with pain in different ways. That is why two people living in the same house can experience similar events and respond differently.

Let's take a moment to look at some of the major ways in which people attempt to deal with pain and the resulting negative emotions.

## Ignore It

Some seek to deal with pain by ignoring it. The thought is that if the negative feelings are ignored they will go away. If only you think good thoughts you won't experience the bad thoughts.

Lana and her five-year-old daughter, Nancy, are sitting in the living room playing with dolls. Harold, Lana's husband, walks in the room and trips on one of the dolls.

"What are you trying to do, kill me?" Harold shouts as he picks up the doll and slams it against the wall. He walks over to Nancy and slaps her face. Nancy's head whips back and she starts to cry.

Harold turns. As he walks through the door, he shouts, "Don't let it happen again or you'll get worse."

Lana grabs Nancy and holds her close. She whispers softly into her ear, "Let's think good thoughts. Why don't we think about going to the beach and building a sand castle. Wouldn't that be fun?"

Lana seeks to distract her daughter with good thoughts. If we think good thoughts everything will go away. If we think about the beach, then the pain of the moment will leave. Ignoring pain will not make it go away.

## Stuff It

Another classic way to deal with pain is to stuff it. This is similar to ignoring pain but is more aggressive. It is not a tactic to deny pain, but a willful attempt to force the pain away though will power.

You know there is an issue that needs to be dealt with in your life. It is affecting you negatively and causing you grief. It is too painful to think about. Every time you allow the pain to surface nothing happens except you feel more miserable and more hopeless that things will ever change.

Every time something brings the situation to the forefront, it is like a scab being ripped off a wound. The pain comes rushing in. You make the herculean effort to stuff it down. You are not ignoring it, you are are willfully pushing it away into the depth of your soul so you don't have to feel the pain.

This takes an incredible amount of effort on your part. It consumes a lot of energy and can begin to affect you not only emotionally but physically. The more things you stuff, the bigger the time bomb waiting to explode. Stuffing pain will never make it go away.

## Accept It

Some people accept pain as a way of life. You grow up with a string of bad events where people have hurt you over and over again. You begin to think that this is your lot in life. If anything bad is going to happen it is going to happen to you.

You feel like you are walking around with a huge bullseye over your heart and everyone is taking a shot at hitting it. There must be an unseen sign on your back saying "Kick Me", because everyone does. This must just be your lot in life.

You start looking at yourself and figure there must be some reason that all these bad things are happening to you. Something must be wrong with you. You must be a bad person. You must deserve what you get.

Once you start thinking this way you stop trying to change your situation. You don't even try to do things or expect things to be different. You just shake your head and accept whatever comes your way. Accepting pain will not make it go away.

## Rehearse It

Some people rehearse their pain. You are consumed by one or more situations from the past. The situation is never far from you. It is almost like a video in your head that is set to replay over and over again.

You sit around and go over the event and how it has hurt you. You dwell on the event and think of things that you should have said and should have done. You nurse your anger and pain because of what they did to you.

Whenever you come to a person, even a complete stranger, you tell them the story of how you were wronged and hurt. Your whole life centers around an event that happened to you sometime in the past.

I remember talking with one person. She was weeping and telling me about an event that took place in her life. After hearing the story and seeing the pain she was experiencing, I asked when the event took place. I was expecting sometime in the last few months. She told me it happened over thirty years ago.

She was reliving an event that had happened over thirty years ago and experiencing the pain as if it was recent. Rehearsing pain will never make it go away

## Medicate It

This is a common way people choose to deal with pain. You seek to medicate it so you don't feel it. You try to cover up the pain, not by willfully putting it down by stuffing it, but by seeking comfort in other places.

There are so many ways you can medicate your pain. Here are some of the more popular:

- Alcohol and drugs - if you are bombed out of your mind the pain goes away for a while.

- Food - you eat for comfort

- Sex - you seek to fill the void and pain with pornography or one sexual relationship after another

- Gambling - the adrenaline of the game

- Shopping - the pleasure of something new

- Work - keeping busy

- Fantasy - living in another life

- Entertainment - sports, video games, movies, etc.

There are a couple of problems with trying to medicate your pain. First, the relief is only temporary. It only helps for a few short minutes or hours.

Second. It causes more problems than it solves. Many of the things listed above are addictive and can lead you into bondage. Now you have the added weight and guilt associated with addition and a whole new set of pain to deal with. Medicating pain will not get rid of it.

## Emulate it

Instead of dealing with the pain, you emulate it. You choose to walk in the same way as the person who caused you pain. You become the person who hurt you.

Not that you are the person who hurt you, you become just like them. You act the same way they acted. You hurt others the same way they hurt you. You choose, maybe not consciously, to be just like them. I know, because that is what I did.

I grew up in the home of a violent alcoholic. My dad was abusive verbally and physically. He was the nicest guy when sober, but scary when he drank.

I grew up filled with anger. I started to sniff paint, do drugs, and drink alcohol. I would get drunk and pick fights with people I didn't even know. They didn't do anything to me. I was just angry.

I always blamed my dad for my anger. I was angry because he was angry. I was convinced beyond a shadow of a doubt that he caused me to be the way I was.

Imagine my surprise. One day after an outburst of anger I started blaming my dad for my anger. I heard the Lord say to me, "You chose to emulate him." I was absolutely shocked. Those words hit me hard and they were the beginning point of my deliverance from anger.

I knew that I could no longer blame my dad for who I was. I chose to be the way I was. Emulating the cause of pain will never get rid of it.

## Bring It to Jesus

Do you use one of these six ways to try and deal with the pain you experience in life?

- Are you ignoring it and hoping everything will be alright?

- Are you stuffing it deep inside so you don't have to feel it or deal with it?

- Are you accepting it and just believing that life always has to be this way for you?

- Are you constantly rehearsing it and experiencing the pain over and over and over again?

- Are you trying to medicate it and making you life more painful in the process?

- Are you emulating the person who hurt you and hurting others in the same way?

If so, it is time to acknowledge how you handle your pain, repent and turn from it, and turn to Jesus who heals the brokenhearted.

There is only one effective way for a believer to deal with pain and that is to bring it to Jesus. Jesus has a plan and the power to remove the pain and heal your broken heart. Tomorrow we will learn how to bring our pain to Jesus and get rid of it.

**1. Which one of the six coping mechanisms do you relate to the most? Why?**

**2. Are there other ways you cope that are different than the six listed? What are they and how do they manifest in your life?**

**3. Now look at the effects your responses had on your life. List all the positive and negative effects you find in your responses to question 1 & 2.**

| Positive Effects | Negative Effects |
|---|---|
|  |  |

**4. Does you way of handling pain actually get rid of the pain and leave you healthy and whole inside? Why or why not?**

166

# Week 5 Day 4

# Jesus Knows Your Pain

## Jesus is Your Healer

Jesus knows your pain. Jesus bore your pain on the cross. But even better than that, Jesus can heal your pain.

## Jesus Knows Your Pain

So often you may feel that no one understands your pain. You tell your story and people glibly say, "Just get over it," or "You need to forgive and forget." But the pain is real and as we have already learned ignoring it doesn't make it go away.

But there is one who does know you pain. Jesus knows your pain. He knows exactly what you are going through. He knows you at a level that no one else in the world can know or understand.

Jesus experienced great depths of pain in His life. We already mentioned the intense emotional struggle he went through in the garden. Here are a few of the things He experienced:

- **Betrayal** - Judas betrayed Jesus for thirty pieces of silver.

- **Abandonment** - All of His disciples fled when they arrested Him in the garden.

- **Denial** - Jesus warned Peter that he would deny him three time before the rooster crowed, and he did.

- **Injustice** - The trials Jesus went through on the night He was betrayed were illegal according to Jewish law.

- **Slander** - The leaders said that He was possessed by the devil and casting out demons by the power of the devil. They brought false witnesses to find some excuse to put Jesus to death,

- **Rejection** - The religious leaders and people rejected Jesus as Messiah and chanted for him to be crucified.

- **Physical Abuse** - The soldiers beat him, plucked out pieces of his beard, placed a crown of thorns on His head and hit it in with a rod, they beat his back with whip thirty-nine times, and they drove nails into His hands and feet as they crucified him on the cross.

- **Mockery** - The soldiers, mocked him by placing a robe upon Him and calling Him king. The leaders and people mocked Him as He was hanging on the cross.

- **The Weight of Sin** - When Jesus hung on the cross the sin of the world was placed on Him. The point of the crucifixion was that Jesus would bear the full penalty for your sin. He who knew no sin became sin for you.

- **The Wrath of God** - The full weight of God's wrath was placed upon Jesus on the cross. God's righteous anger and judgment were centered on Jesus as a sacrifice for all.

All of these things show how Jesus can relate to your pain. But there is even a greater way that He understands your pain. He is God and knows all things. He knows you. He knows your thoughts and feelings. He understands exactly what you are going through to the slightest detail.

I am sitting with Dennis and Gayle, a very distraught young couple, who just lost their newborn baby. The father is sobbing and shaking his head back and forth. He could not believe that his baby boy just died. I say gently to the couple, "I can somewhat understand what you are going through."

The words are barely out of my mouth and the father's head snaps up. His eyes glare at me and he vehemently says, "You don't understand how we feel. I am sick and tired of people telling me that they know what I feel. You don't know what I am feeling."

"No, I don't know exactly what you are feeling," I say, "but my wife and I lost our first son." The hardness of his eyes softens and he tilts forward open to receive my story.

"My wife is seven months pregnant and her water breaks. They rush her to the hospital and she gives birth to Zachariah Lee, we call him Zach."

"I couldn't be there for Zach's birth because I was in Basic Training for the Air Force in Texas. At mail call that day my Training Instructor made the announcement that Airman Tuinder is the father of a new baby boy. I was shocked and so happy I could hardly stand it."

"The next day another Instructor called me into the office and told me that my son was dead and that he was there to help go through the paperwork to go home on emergency leave. My heart is broken. My son's dead. My wife is 1,427 miles away."

"After what seems like a million years I arrive home. I walk in the bedroom where my wife is recovering. I run to her, grab her into my arms, and we weep together. She tells me that Zach lived less than twenty-four hours. The doctor did all he could do but his lungs collapsed and he died.

168

"The first and only time I meet Zach was at his funeral. He is lying in a tiny casket. I walk up and look at him. He is lying there so peacefully. I run my hand over his hair and giggle, because his hair was longer than mine."

"No, I can't understand exactly the pain you are going through, but I do know the pain of losing a baby."

Maybe no one around you understands the pain you are experiencing, but Jesus does. You may think that you have to bear this pain alone, but you don't. **You can bring your pain to Jesus.** Jesus took your pain upon Himself on the cross so you don't have to bear it.

## Jesus Bore Your Pain

**Surely our griefs He Himself bore,**
**And our sorrows He carried;**
**Yet we ourselves esteemed Him stricken,**
**Smitten of God, and afflicted.**
**But He was pierced through**
**for our transgressions,**
**He was crushed for our iniquities;**
**The chastening for our well-being fell upon Him,**
**And by His scourging we are healed.**
**(Isaiah 53:4-5)**

The first two lines of verse four tell you that Jesus bore or carried your griefs and sorrows. He took them upon Himself when He went to the cross.

Both the word griefs and sorrows (note they are plural) carry the idea of physical and emotional sickness or anguish. Jesus bore your physical and emotional anguish on the cross.

We already mentioned that emotions are okay and that God gave them to us. When bad things happen to you, you should expect to experience pain, but pain is only meant to be temporary. There should be an end to the pain.

It's when pain is allowed to linger that trouble begins. Unresolved emotional pain has been known to cause physical illnesses, relationship problems, and personal inner struggles. You are not created by God to bear long-term emotional pain. Jesus came to bear your emotional pain and distress.

## Jesus Can Heal Your Pain

**". . . He has sent me to bind up the brokenhearted**
**. . . " (Isaiah 61:1)**

**"He heals the brokenhearted, and binds up their**
**wounds." (Psalm 147:3)**

**"The Lord is near to the brokenhearted, and
saves those who are crushed in spirit."
(Psalm 34:18)**

**"He restores my soul . . ." (Psalm 23:3)**

This is the great part of the story. You don't have to remain in pain. God sent Jesus to bind up your broken heart. Are you willing to bring your pain to Jesus?

During the retreat, God is going to to a great job of breaking through years of pain to bring healing to areas of your broken heart. The main thing is for you to come to the retreat with a willing heart determined to gain your freedom and healing no matter what.

**1. Get before the Lord and let Him know of your willingness to let Him into the painful areas of your heart. In the area below write to the Lord your intentions as you prepare to participate in the retreat.**

**2. What areas would you like the Lord to heal?**

# Week 5 Day 5

# Preparing for the Retreat

Fantastic! You've made it this far and are pressing in toward the goal. Remember, the retreat is the most important part of the EHV Seminar and Retreat. You have received a ton of information over the past five weeks and now it is time to put it all into practice and receive some major breakthroughs in your life.

I've been involved in deliverance ministry since 1997 and have personally lead over 100 retreats. In every retreat I see the Lord moving powerfully and setting people free. The same will happen in your life as you press in to receive all that the Lord has for you.

Here's some simple advice as you prepare your heart for the upcoming retreat.

## Expect Resistance

I'm not saying this to scare you. I'm saying it because the enemy will do whatever he can do to stop you from attending the retreat. Stand up against everything that gets in the way. Resist the devil and he will flee from you.

I'm not saying this will happen to you, but if it does you will know where it comes from. You may wake and feel too sick to go the retreat or one of your kids is sick. You may get in a big fight right before the retreat or on the way to the retreat. Chaos may hit your home during the week of the retreat.

In every case it is the work of the enemy trying to distract you from the retreat. If you find some of these things happening call your seminar leaders and agree together in prayer. Stand up to the devil and resist him. Press in and get to the retreat.

## Come Expecting, I Am

God graciously led you to attend the seminar so that He could lead you into His paths of freedom. Come expecting God to do something great in your life. He loves you so much and is for you.

He will do wonderful things that you cannot even imagine. In one of the videos, I mentioned how God delivered me from a Spirit of murder. I never thought that I could be free from the rage that rose in my chest every time I was angry. But God delivered me. I had peace in my life that I did not know existed. Something similar will happen in your life too. Come expecting.

## Open You Heart to the Lord

I also want to encourage you to open your heart to the Lord and let Him come in and heal the broken areas of your life. God loves you deeply and wants to heal your broken heart. Recognize that the way you have been dealing with pain has not worked and invite Jesus to come and heal your wounds.

Jesus knows your pain, has experienced your pain, and bore your pain upon the cross. If painful memories arise during the retreat don't Ignore or stuff them. Bring them to the Lord and ask Him to take them. Release the pain to Jesus and everyone who caused the pain.

Turn them both over to Jesus to do with them as He desires. He already bore your pain. He already bore the sin done against you. Let Him take the pain and give you the healing your heart desires.

## Trust the Ministry Team

Everyone on the ministry team has sat where you are sitting and gone through at least two seminars and retreats and felt called to be a part of the ministry team. They have been approved by pastoral leadership and trained in effective deliverance ministry prior to the retreat.

When it is time for you to receive ministry accept the next person open to minister to you as a gift from the Lord. Be open and allow them to guide you in the deliverance steps for each topic of the retreat. Trust the Lord and receive His blessings.

# Week 6

## Receive God's Blessings

### This Week's Goals

- To review the concept of the Eight Steps of Experiencing His Victory.

- To gain an understanding of the concept of blessings.

- To understand the scope of God's blessings and His desire for you to experience them.

- To recognize and put into practice various actions that will ensure your continued growth and freedom in Christ.

# Week 6 Teaching Notes

## An Overview of the Eight Steps

1. Examine Your Relationship with God

2. Ask God for Revelation

3. Take Responsibility for Your Own Actions

4. Repent and Turn to God

5. Renounce and Turn from Sin

6. Let Jesus Restore Your Soul

7. Repulse the Enemy

8. Receive God's Blessings

Good Fortune
Vitality
Health
Longevity
Fertility
Numerous Offspring

Deuteronomy 28:1-14

## Basic Concepts of Blessing

Blessings always start with God

James 1:16-17

Blessings are spoken to people.

Blessings are speaking God's intentions for others.

Blessings are a conduit for God's Grace.

Blessings always release increase and abundance.

Blessings endues a person with power to succeed.

God wants to bless you.

## God's Daily Blessing from Numbers

Numbers 6:22-27

The Lord Bless You

The Lord Keep You

The Lord Make His
Face Shine Upon You

The Lord Be Gracious
to You

The Lord Lift Up His
Countenance Upon You

The Lord Give You
Peace

## Steps to Continued Freedom

1. Expect the devil to return

Matthew 12:43-53

2. Expect to be tempted

Matthew 4:1
Luke 4:13

3. Be Aggressive against the enemy

4. Daily review the truths God showed you

5. Identify and change any habits or issues of the flesh

6. Hang out with those who are pursuing God

7. Share your testimony

178

## Steps to Continued Freedom

8. Invite someone to the next Seminar and Retreat

9. Keep going over the materials in this study

10. Go through the Who You Are in Christ video series

11. Get baptized

12. Be an active part of a local church

13. Get in the word of God

14. Live a lifestyle of repentance

# Class Discussion

1. What part of the teaching made the greatest impact on your life today?

2. Do you have any questions about the retreat or testimonies you would like to share from the retreat?

3. Step 8 is about receiving God's blessings. What are the key lessons you learned about blessings?

4. One of the key parts of the retreat is when the prayer minister and retreat leader spoke a blessing over you. Describe the impact this had on your life.

5. What are some concrete things you can do to ensure that you receive all the blessing God has for your life?

6. Do any of the suggestions on how to keep your freedom stand out to you? If so, why?

7. If you could wrap the most important things that you have learned from this retreat into one or two statements, what would they be?

# Week 6 Day 1

# What is a Blessing Anyway?

Someone sneezes and even a complete stranger will say, "Bless you" or "God bless you." Many people say a blessing before they eat their food. God had the priests speak a blessing over the children of Israel. At the end of his life, Jacob blessed his children. Jesus blessed the little children. So the question we are going to answer today is what is a blessing anyway?

The general concept is easy to describe. Take this simple dictionary definition: "God's favor and protection." Simple. Straightforward. Easy. But as with most concepts, there is a depth of meaning that can be found if we are willing to take the time to dig deeper.

## All Blessings Start with God

God is the creator of all that exists. He created the heavens and the earth and all that is in it. He spoke everything into existence until it came to the creation of man. Instead of speaking the man into existence, God formed man out of the dust of the ground and breathed life into him and he became a living being (Genesis 2:8).

The very first recorded words in the Bible that God spoke to man was a blessing. Genesis 1:28 says,

> **God blessed them (Adam and Eve); and God said
> to them, "Be fruitful and multiply, and fill the
> earth, and subdue it; and rule over the fish of the
> sea, and over the birds of the sky and over every
> living thing that moves on the earth.**

God creates man in His image and gives them the authority to rule the earth. This rule was to be conducted through a personal relationship with Him. Man is created out of the love of God to love Him and rule with Him.

So it only makes sense that God desires for man to flourish and experience his favor and protection. He wants Adam and Eve to grow into the fullness of life as He intends it to be. This is as it should be since,

> **Every good thing given and every perfect gift is
> from above, coming down from the Father of
> lights, with whom there is no variation or shifting
> shadow. (James 1:17)**

Recognizing that God's love is the wellspring of every blessing is foundational. God loves you with an everlasting love and wants to pour out His blessings upon you.

## Blessings are Spoken to People

There's power in words. God spoke words and creation came into existence. The Bible tells us that we can speak words that will bring life to people and words that will bring death.

**Death and life are in the power of the tongue, And those who love it will eat its fruit. (Proverbs 18:21)**

Blessings are very similar to prayer. The difference is that in praying we speak to God and in blessing we speak to people.

A blessing is more than kind thoughts toward a person. A blessing is more than a prayer lifted up to God in your mind. A blessing is a spoken word said in the presence of the person(s) being blessed.

## Blessings are Speaking God's Intentions for Others

A blessing is not the kind intentions that we have toward a person and what we want to happen in their life. It is a declaration of God's intent toward a person.

Since God is the source of all blessing, we must go to Him to find out what His intentions are toward the person we want to bless. In one sense a blessing is very similar to a prophecy.

Prophecy is more direct where it says what the Lord will do, whereas, blessings are what God wants to do in a person's life. The reason I say wants to do and not will do is that we can short-circuit what God desires to do in our lives through disobedience.

God has immeasurable riches He desires to pour out upon you. These riches are only available as you learn to walk in His ways

## Blessings are a Conduit for God's Grace

Frank Dimazzio speaks of a blessing as a "transmission or endowment of the power of God's goodness and favor poured into my life." When we speak a blessing over a person, it opens the door for God to work in their lives as only He can do.

Another way to describe it is to say that when we bless someone we are directing God's goodness to them. We are inviting God's power to show up in their lives to bring about a change in their situation.

Nelson's New Illustrated Bible Dictionary says a blessing is,

182

**The act of declaring, or wishing, favor and goodness upon others. The blessing is not only for the good effect of the words; it also has the power to bring that to pass.**

Once we understand that God is the source of all blessing and we have received a blessing from Him for a person, we can be assured that He has the desire and ability to carry it out in the life of the person we blessed.

## Blessings Always Release Increase

The first phrase in God's blessing of Adam and Eve is "Be fruitful and multiply." Both of these terms signify a great increase. God desires to pour out His blessings in ways that will astound us. He is the God who is able to do exceedingly, abundantly more than we can ask or think (Ephesians 3:20).

I found this great definition in the Theological Wordbook of the Old Testament,

**To endue with power for success, prosperity, fecundity [which means, the ability to produce an abundance of offspring or new growth], longevity, etc;**

God wants you to experience the fullness of His blessing in every area of your life. Here are a few of the things He desires for you:

**love, joy, peace, gentleness, kindness, goodness, meekness, patience, eternal life, compassion, mercy, grace, strength, encouragement, freedom, wholeness, support, purpose, meaning, value, hope, gifts, talents, fulfillment, right relationships, blessings, promises, an inheritance, comfort, healing, restoration, reconciliation, unity, harmony, edification, fellowship, communion, soundness of mind, prosperity, abundance, an overflowing cup, generosity, companionship.**

## Two Examples of Blessings

The first blessing comes from Genesis 27:28-29. It is where Isaac thinks he is blessing his son Esau, but in fact is blessing Jacob. Notice how the word "may" is used.

**28 Now may God give you of the dew of heaven, And of the fatness of the earth, And an abundance of grain and new wine; 29 May peoples serve you, And nations bow down to you; Be master of your brothers,**

**And may your mother's sons bow down to you.
Cursed be those who curse you.
And blessed be those who bless you."**

The second example is the blessing that God commands Aaron to speak over the children of Israel. This blessing doesn't use the word may. It simply speaks what the Lord desires to take place in their lives. God calls it invoking His name on the sons of Israel.

**22 Then the Lord spoke to Moses, saying, 23
"Speak to Aaron and to his sons, saying, 'Thus
you shall bless the sons of Israel.
You shall say to them:
24 The Lord bless you, and keep you;
25 The Lord make His face shine on you,
And be gracious to you;
26 The Lord lift up His countenance on you,
And give you peace.'
27 So they shall invoke My name on the sons of
Israel, and I then will bless them.
(Numbers 6:22-27)**

Tomorrow we will look at this last blessing in more detail to help us understand how the Lord wants to bless His people.

## My Blessing For You

Before you go I would like to speak a blessing over you:

May the Lord open your eyes to the greatness of who He is.
May you understand all the richness of His blessing.
May you receive a revelation of the importance of speaking blessings.
May He give you insight into how you can speak blessings into the lives of others.
May He give you ample opportunity to speak His blessings to those around you.
May you abound in the things of the Lord and increase in His favor

## 1. After reading the above article, how would you define God's blessings?

# Week 6 Day 2

# The Anatomy of a Blessing

I'm very fired up about the whole topic of blessings. Studying It has stirred up something in my heart that I pray grows and continues. I want to be a person who experiences the full blessing of the Lord in my life. I also want to be a person who blesses others in the name of the Lord so they can experience life as God intends it to be.

I've said this my whole adult life, God is good. I said it even before I came to know the Lord. I said it to my family and friends who were at the graveside service for Suzette and my son, Zachariah Lee, who was born premature and lived for only one day.

So here I was, an unbeliever, telling all those who would listen that God is good. I told them not to blame God for Zach's death because God is good. Have I said it enough? Probably not. God is good. God is good. God is good. God is good.

## God Wants to Bless You

God is in the business of blessing. God is love and so it is natural for Him to want to pour out His blessings on His people. God wants to bless you.

As we saw last week, God is the source of all blessing. Everything good flows from Him.

God wanted to make sure that His people knew His heart toward them. He told Moses to have Aaron bless His children every day of the year. He commanded Aaron and his sons (the priests) to bless them at the close of the daily service.

Let's look at the passage and then break down the anatomy of God's blessing to see what it entails. Numbers 6:22-27 says:

**22 Then the Lord spoke to Moses, saying, 23
"Speak to Aaron and to his sons, saying, 'Thus
you shall bless the sons of Israel.
You shall say to them:
24 The Lord bless you, and keep you;
25 The Lord make His face shine on you,
And be gracious to you;
26 The Lord lift up His countenance on you,
And give you peace.'
27 So they shall invoke My name on the sons of
Israel, and I then will bless them."**

Notice that it is God who is the one who initiates the blessing. That is awesome because He is the one who created us and knows us the best. If anyone knows how to bless it is God. That is why we want to take this blessing apart piece by piece to see what God is speaking about.

## The Anatomy of a Blessing

There are six main themes to God's blessing. Before we look at them I want to share a couple of fun ideas. The first is the word LORD is the personal name of God which was revealed to Moses when God called him to bring the children of Israel out of Egypt: Yahweh.

The second is Yahweh is used three times in this blessing. Some see the three members of the Trinity in the repetition of the name of God three times. The Father blesses and keeps us, while the Son gives His presence and is gracious toward us, and the Holy Spirit pays attention to us and brings us peace. How exciting.

So let's take a moment and look at each of the six aspects of blessing that God wants you to experience from Him on a daily basis. Remember, this blessing was to be spoken on a daily basis to the children of Israel for life.

In other words, God wants to bless you with these things each and every new day of your life.

## The Lord Bless You

We covered the concept of blessing yesterday in *What is a Blessing Anyway?*, but I want to hit the highlights again this week:

All blessings start with God. He is the one who initiated this blessing, not Moses or Aaron.

Blessings are spoken to people. That is why God was having Aaron and his sons speak this over the people daily.

Blessings are speaking God's intentions for another. He wants the people to know His intentions toward them.

Blessings are a conduit of God's grace. God's mercies are new every morning and He wants us to experience His blessings daily.

Blessings always bring increase. He wants us to experience His presence and abundant life.

Are you sensing that God is for you and He only wants what is best for you? Are you starting to realize that God has already made all His blessings available to you and is waiting to pour them out on you?

186

## The Lord Keep You

The main concept behind this word is God is exercising great care over you. The idea is guarding or keeping in a careful, diligent way. He is always watching over you. This concept brings two passages to my mind that speak of God's great care for you.

The first passage is Psalm 121:1-8. It reads,

> 1 I will lift up my eyes to the mountains;
> From where shall my help come?
> 2 My help comes from the Lord,
> Who made heaven and earth.
> 3 He will not allow your foot to slip;
> He who keeps you will not slumber.
> 4 Behold, He who keeps Israel
> Will neither slumber nor sleep.
>
> 5 The Lord is your keeper;
> The Lord is your shade on your right hand.
> 6 The sun will not smite you by day,
> Nor the moon by night.
> 7 The Lord will protect you from all evil;
> He will keep your soul.
> 8 The Lord will guard your going out
> and your coming in
> From this time forth and forever.

The second is Psalm 23:1-6. It says:

> 1 The Lord is my shepherd,
> I shall not want.
> 2 He makes me lie down in green pastures;
> He leads me beside quiet waters.
> 3 He restores my soul;
> He guides me in the paths of righteousness
> For His name's sake.
>
> 4 Even though I walk through the valley of the
> shadow of death,
> I fear no evil, for You are with me;
> Your rod and Your staff, they comfort me.
> 5 You prepare a table before me in
> the presence of my enemies;
> You have anointed my head with oil;
> My cup overflows.
> 6 Surely goodness and lovingkindness will follow
> me all the days of my life,
> And I will dwell in the house of the Lord forever.

Even in the midst of the valley of the shadow of death, God is with us and will protect us with His staff and rod.

## The Lord Make His Face Shine on You

This phrase has a lot of meaning to it. Face speaks of God's presence. Of course, you don't get to see God's face, but Moses could speak to God as a man speaks face to face. God would descend in a cloud and speak with Moses. The idea is that God wants you to experience His presence on a daily basis.

You always have the promise that God will never leave you or forsake you, but this is more than just His presence in our life. It speaks of His Divine approval and goodwill toward you. God is looking for an intimate relationship with you.

Again this speaks of His favor. This is the same word that Gabriel spoke to Mary when he greeted her. He said, "Do not be afraid, Mary; for you have found favor with God" (Luke 1:30). It is also the same word that speaks of Jesus increasing in favor with God and men (Luke 2:52). Isn't it wonderful that God is pouring out the same blessing upon you as He did on Jesus?

## The Lord Be Gracious to You

This is a fantastic word in which God describes His desire to show an act of kindness, compassion, or benefice to another. It is God's heartfelt response to you. He has what you need and He wants you to receive it.

God shows His graciousness out of His giving nature. It's not something that can be earned. If it was earned it would be your due. What the Lord is clearly saying is that He wants to give you gifts of grace that are sourced out of Him and His abundance.

God is a God of grace. He gives you precious gifts that you could never deserve or earn.

So often I hear people say they don't deserve anything from God because of the way they have lived their life. They are so used to earning things and know they don't deserve what God is giving.

Yet God values you so much that He is willing to give you things you don't deserve. He sees value in you that you don't see in yourself. He sees you as you really are, not just the actions you have taken. He wants to pour out His grace on you in ever increasing ways.

## The Lord Lift Up His Countenance on You

This phrase has a different focus than the previous one. It deals with God's presence and His attitude toward you. This phrase focuses on the idea of God paying attention to you. He is looking for you. An interesting point some of the word study experts point out is that this phrase also connotes that God is looking at you and smiling.

188

Do you ever think that God is pleased with you and when He sees you He smiles? God loves you. You are His child. He looks at you and rejoices.

When Jesus was baptized by John God said, "This is My beloved Son, in whom I am well-pleased." (Matthew 3:17). I know, you might be thinking, "Yeah, but that's Jesus. There is no way God is pleased with me." Oh yeah.

If you are living in a way that is not pleasing to the Lord, He is there every single day of your life with every spiritual blessing you need for life and godliness. He desires to turn His face to you and help you in your time of need, You are never helpless or hopeless for God is looking and there to help.

## The Lord Give You Peace

The more I study the word Shalom (peace), the more excited I get about it. This word is so much more than the English word peace means. It is used in the Old Testament 250 times.

The basic idea behind it is massive and impacts every part of a person's life. The very foundation of this word means completion and fulfillment. It means prosperity, wellness, health, completeness, safety, and satisfaction. Are you getting the breadth of this word?

It is used in the Bible as a greeting and as a way to say goodbye. "To wish someone shalom implies a blessing . . . to withhold shalom implies a curse." This is an important concept.

Nearly two-thirds of the usages of shalom "describes the state of fulfillment which is the result of God's presence."

This is how God wants you to live in the abundance of His provision. This is what He speaks over you day after day.

## Invoke My Name

God said Aaron and his sons would invoke His name on the people and He would bless them. Invoking the name of God means to call upon Him to do this blessing. He is the only one who has the ability and the resources to bless you.

It seems to be quite a simple thing. If you will invoke His name, He will bless. Look around you. Everywhere you go there are people God desires to bless. He even encourages you to bless your enemies and those who do you harm.

Remember, God takes no joy in bringing judgment to anyone in the world. He sent His Son Jesus to pay for the sins of the world. You are to be a blesser and not a curser.

**1. God wants to bless you.  What feelings and thoughts come to your mind when you hear those words?**

**2. God wants you to be a person who releases His blessings on others. Think of someone close to you. Ask the Lord to give you a blessing specifically for them. Write it down below and then contact the person and bless them. Tell them you are learning about blessings and would like to speak one over them. (see and example at the end of Week 6 Day 3)**

# Week 6 Day 3
# The Incredible Extent of God's Blessing

I think it is hard to imagine all the blessings that God desires to pour out upon His people. After all, He is the one who "is able to do exceedingly abundantly above all that we ask or think" (Ephesians 3:20).

God's heart is for you and He has plans for you that are amazing. There is no doubt in my mind that God wants to bless you.

> **1 "Now it shall be, if you diligently obey the Lord your God, being careful to do all His commandments which I command you today, the Lord your God will set you high above all the nations of the earth. 2 All these blessings will come upon you and overtake you if you obey the Lord your God (Deuteronomy 28:1-2)**

There's a perfect passage of Scripture that speaks of the manifold blessings that the Lord wants to give to His people. It comes from Deuteronomy chapter twenty-eight where Moses gathers the children of Israel and tells them of the all the blessings that will come upon them as they enter into the promised land if they obey God's ways and the curses that will come upon them if they don't.

So what are the blessings God is talking about? He lists them in Deuteronomy 28:3-14:

> **3 "Blessed shall you be in the city, and blessed shall you be in the country.**
> **4 "Blessed shall be the offspring of your body and the produce of your ground and the offspring of your beasts, the increase of your herd and the young of your flock.**
> **5 "Blessed shall be your basket and your kneading bowl.**
> **6 "Blessed shall you be when you come in, and blessed shall you be when you go out.**
>
> **7 "The Lord shall cause your enemies who rise up against you to be defeated before you; they will come out against you one way and will flee before you seven ways. 8 The Lord will command the blessing upon you in your barns and in all that you put your hand to, and He will bless you in the land which the Lord your God gives you.**

**9 The Lord will establish you as a holy people to Himself, as He swore to you, if you keep the commandments of the Lord your God and walk in His ways. 10 So all the peoples of the earth will see that you are called by the name of the Lord, and they will be afraid of you. 11 The Lord will make you abound in prosperity, in the offspring of your body and in the offspring of your beast and in the produce of your ground, in the land which the Lord swore to your fathers to give you. 12 The Lord will open for you His good storehouse, the heavens, to give rain to your land in its season and to bless all the work of your hand; and you shall lend to many nations, but you shall not borrow. 13 The Lord will make you the head and not the tail, and you only will be above, and you will not be underneath, if you listen to the commandments of the Lord your God, which I charge you today, to observe them carefully, 14 and do not turn aside from any of the words which I command you today, to the right or to the left, to go after other gods to serve them.**

## God's Blessings Come Through Doing Things His Way

Since God is your creator He knows what is best for you. He knows the things that will cause you to grow and increase and prosper. He also knows that things that will hinder your growth, bring decrease, and lead you to poverty.

God has graciously given you knowledge of His ways and the wisdom you need to live life to the fullest. His commandments are for your good. A lot of people look at His commandments as a list of restrictions seeking to hinder their freedom and keep them from experiencing life. But, quite to the contrary, they are the things that ensure you can experience life as God intends it to be.

For example, every piece of equipment I get comes with a manual telling me about my product and telling me the best practices to keep it running at its best. My car manual tells me the type of gas I should use, how often to change the oil, the air pressure in my tires, and a ton of other instructions.

Why in the world are there so many instructions? I just want to drive my car.

Do you know what would happen if I filled my car that uses unleaded gas with diesel fuel? It would run for a while and then slowly deteriorate as the fuel injectors, filters, and fuel lines clog up. If left this way the diesel fuel could damage the engine and I would not be able to drive my car any longer.

Why does the manufacturer only allow a certain kind of fuel? Why are they so restrictive? The commonsense answer is that the engine was created to use unleaded fuel. If you want it to work right you must follow the commandments of the manufacturer.

I'm sure you see the parallel. God is your creator and He created you a certain way. If you desire to have a life that runs to its full potential, then you need to listen closely to the Creator's instructions. God's commandments are for your good and ensure the blessings of God in your life.

## God's Blessings Will Pursue You

I love how verse two pictures the results of obeying God. Moses says that if you obey God all these blessings will come upon you and overtake you.

If you walk in God's way, you are assured that the blessings will come to you. They will arrive in due season. They will overtake you. The word is used to describe someone who is chasing after someone to catch up with them.

Can you picture in your mind all the blessings you just read in the passage above running after you and catching up to you because you are doing things God's way? Well you should, it's what Moses is saying.

## The Scope of God's Blessings

### Prosperity

The first part of verse eleven says, "The LORD will make you abound in prosperity." It doesn't matter if you live in the country or in a city, God will make you prosper. It carries the idea of whatever is "good, pleasant, beautiful, delightful, glad, joyful, precious, correct, righteous" (TWOT). It's everything God wants to pour out upon you.

God wants to bless the offspring of your body, the produce of the ground, the offspring of your beasts and herds. If you are not a farmer or rancher, then God wants to bless the work of your hands. He wants to bless you in your job and see you increase.

Whatever you put your hand to, God will send blessings to catch up and overtake you.

The story that comes to mind is that of Joseph. His brothers sell him into slavery and he sold to Potiphar. Potiphar senses the presence of God on his life and places Joseph in charge of everything he owns.

Joseph is them falsely accused and cast into prison. The chief jailer senses the presence of the Lord upon Joseph and he is promoted to run the things in the prison.

Then one day Joseph is called out of the prison to tell Pharaoh the interpretation of his dream and suggestions on how to prepare because of it. He is elevated to the second-in-command of Egypt. That is definitely a story of prospering wherever you may be, whether in bad or good situations.

## Protection

The Lord promises His protection against your enemies. All the plotting and planning of your enemies will come to naught. They will come in one way, but God will send them out seven ways.

The one who comes to mind is David. The shepherd boy who slew Goliath and sent the Philistine army fleeing for their lives. He was soon the one fleeing for his own life as King Saul sought to kill him out of jealousy and fear of losing his kingdom to David.

Many times in the Psalms, David cried out for help from the Lord. Even when he was in the depth of despair he would lift his eyes to the Lord and declare His trust in Him. In Psalm 28:7-9, David says:

> **7 The Lord is my strength and my shield;**
> **My heart trusts in Him, and I am helped;**
> **Therefore my heart exults,**
> **And with my song I shall thank Him.**
> **8 The Lord is their strength,**
> **And He is a saving defense to His anointed.**
> **9 Save Your people and bless Your inheritance;**
> **Be their shepherd also, and carry them forever.**

## Spiritual Well-Being

Moses reveals that part of the incredible blessings of the Lord is that you are part of the Lord's people. He says in verse 9, "The LORD will establish you as a holy people to Himself, as He swore to you."

You are part of the people of God and hold a special relationship with Him that the world doesn't have. You are called to be holy or set apart to Him. In your love and trust in God, you walk in His ways.

An interesting thing takes place. As you walk in God's ways His blessings come upon you and other people see and they glorify God. All the people of the earth will recognize that you are a part of the Lord's people.

This reminds me of the story of King Solomon who requested from God wisdom to lead the people. God gave Him wisdom and riches so great that the people came from all over the world to marvel at his understanding and learn from him. Listen to the story in 1 Kings 10:1-10:

> **1 Now when the queen of Sheba heard about the**
> **fame of Solomon concerning the name of the**
> **Lord, she came to test him with difficult**
> **questions. 2 So she came to Jerusalem with a**
> **very large retinue, with camels carrying spices**

and very much gold and precious stones. When she came to Solomon, she spoke with him about all that was in her heart. 3 Solomon answered all her questions; nothing was hidden from the king which he did not explain to her. 4 When the queen of Sheba perceived all the wisdom of Solomon, the house that he had built, 5 the food of his table, the seating of his servants, the attendance of his waiters and their attire, his cupbearers, and his stairway by which he went up to the house of the Lord, there was no more spirit in her. 6 Then she said to the king, "It was a true report which I heard in my own land about your words and your wisdom. 7 Nevertheless I did not believe the reports, until I came and my eyes had seen it. And behold, the half was not told me. You exceed in wisdom and prosperity the report which I heard. 8 How blessed are your men, how blessed are these your servants who stand before you continually and hear your wisdom. 9 Blessed be the Lord your God who delighted in you to set you on the throne of Israel; because the Lord loved Israel forever, therefore He made you king, to do justice and righteousness." 10 She gave the king a hundred and twenty talents of gold, and a very great amount of spices and precious stones. Never again did such abundance of spices come in as that which the queen of Sheba gave King Solomon.

You are a marked person. God wants to pour out His blessings at every level of your life so that people will see the effects and come and seek the wisdom and blessing of the Lord.

## Prominence

Moses says it a couple of different ways. If you choose to follow after God, He will make you prosper to the point that others will recognize the hand of the Lord upon you and hold you in esteem. Remember Joseph.

The idea of you being exalted is not so you can lord it over others but so you can be a light shining in the darkness and drawing people to Him. Remember Solomon.

This exaltation is not for your personal gain or glory. It is for the glory of the Lord. It is those who are humble before God and submitted to His ways that are exalted. Even Peter understood this and told us in 1 Peter 5:6:

**Therefore humble yourselves under the mighty hand of God, that He may exalt you at the proper time**

God told Israel that if they would follow His ways He would "set [them] on high above all the nations" (v. 2) and they would be "the head and not the tail" (v. 13).

The Lord truly wants to bless and elevate you in the minds of the people around you so that they will be drawn to Him. You may never stand before kings, queens, or presidents, but He can elevate you before the eyes of those with whom you have contact so they will seek you out for help.

I remember I got a job making walk-in freezer and coolers for restaurants. On my breaks, I would read the Bible. One guy saw this and made fun of me. Every day he would mock me before the rest of the crew.

I just ignored him and let him have his fun. I didn't appreciate it much, but what was the point of arguing and making a scene in front of the others?

After I was there a few months, something happened in this man's life. He came back to where I was working humble and broken asking for my help. I gladly sought to help him.

In his time of need, this man knew to come to one who knew the Lord. He saw something in my life and when he was in trouble he sought me out. Remember that people are watching your life. There may come a time when they seek you out because of your witness. This is a time to be a blessing to them.

## My Blessing to You

May the Lord bless you.
May the blessings of the Lord come upon you and overtake you.
May the Lord prosper the work of your hands.
May He protect all that is yours.
May the Lord establish you and give you prominence.
May people be drawn to you and come to the knowledge of the Lord.

**1, Write down ten blessing that the Lord has provided in your life and thank Him for each and every one.**

196

# Week 6 Day 4

# Steps to Continued Freedom 1

**1. Expect the devil to return.** The devil will return and try to reestablish his hold in your life. Reject him and command him to go away. Just as you kicked him out of your life at the retreat, resist him and he will flee from you.

2. **Expect to be tempted.** What can you learn from the fact that after Jesus was tempted by the devil in the wilderness and won that the devil still wanted to wait for an opportune time to tempt him later (see Luke 4:13)?

3. **Be aggressive against the enemy.** Never fear the enemy. Take authority over him and command him out of your life. The Scriptures tell us that we are wrestling against demonic forces. Never give in.

4. **Daily review the truths God showed you.** Go over them again and again reminding yourself what the Lord has said to you. His truth is your life. Put them in your phone. Hang them form your wall. Do what it takes to remind yourself of God's truth. Get it deep in your heart where no one or nothing can touch it.

5. **Identify and change and habits or issues of the flesh.** Jot down some of the areas that you know need to change in your life. Determine to make a plan for each one of them at a later date. Remember your growth in God is a process. If you try to change everything at once you can get overwhelmed. Ask the Lord what He wants you to work on and come up with a plan with Him.

**The things I need to work on with God's help are:**

6. **Hang out with those who are pursuing God.** There may be some people in your life that you can no longer hang out with if you want to grow in the Lord. There are some who will reject your stand and constantly seek to encourage you to sin. You know the ones that drag you down. You are doing great in your walk, then you spend time with them and fall. It may be time to separate from those who drag you down and search for those who are pursuing God and will encourage your walk with God

**Ask the Lord if there someone you need to stop hanging out with. Ask the Lord if there someone you need to spend more time with because they are pursuing God.**

7. **Share your testimony.** Let people know the good things that God is doing in your life. Use wisdom in how much detail to share, but let people know the wonderful things the Lord has done for you.

# Week 6 Day 5

# Steps to Continued Freedom 2

8. **Invite someone to the next seminar and retreat.** If God has touched you mightily, why not share it with another friend. Tell them about the retreat and tell them you will go through it with them. You get more out of the second time than the first. It will be a win-win situation.

9. **Keep going over the materials in the is study.** My hope is that you will use this workbook over and over until you get the material it teaches down in your heart. The eight steps can help you walk through any situation in your life that is getting in the way of your growth in Christ. Learn the steps and walk through them on a regular basis.

10. **Go through the Who You Are in Christ video series.** This series is available for free on the Experiencing His Victory Academy. You will have to opt into the free membership level to gain access to them. You can find out more information at www.experiencinghisvictory.com/academy

11. **Get baptized.** Jesus was baptized and calls all believers to be baptized. It is a powerful work of God's grace. Baptism makes a public statement that you are repenting and becoming a follower of Jesus Christ. Going under the water represents your dying to sin and coming up out of the water represents your resurrection into a new life of following God.

**12. Be an active part of a local church**. If you want to grow in your relationship with the Lord, you must be an active part of a local church. The church is God's Idea and that is the place He has designed to help you grow in Christ.

You grow in the Lord by living with a group of believers that are seeking to grow in the things of God. You grow by serving others.

Just remember that no church is perfect. Each one is filled with imperfect people.

**13. Get in the word of God.** It is vital that you become a person of the word. God's word contains the truths you need to grow close to God. God's word is your guide and will help you walk in the truth and experience the fullness that God has made available through Jesus Christ.

Start where you are. If you have never read the Bible before, then try and read a chapter a day. Realize that at first it may seem difficult to understand. Ask the Holy Spirit to help you understand the Bible. Ask those who know the Bible better than you any questions you might have. The more you learn the more you will want to learn.

**14. Practice a lifestyle of repentance.** Make it your purpose to be a quick repenter. If you recognize something sinful in your life, repent immediately, turn to God, and be forgiven. Don't allow things to build up. When something comes to your attention, deal with it immediately and reestablish your walk with the Lord.

# About the Author

Terry L. Tuinder is blessed to be married to his wife, Suzette; to have a wonderful son and daughter-in-law, Josh and Lina; and four fantastic grandchildren, Trinity, Faith, Selah, and Zeal.

Terry accepted Jesus Christ as Lord of his life in May of 1979 while serving at Luke Air Force Base in Phoenix, AZ. He was called into the ministry within six months of coming to the Lord and received a BA from Eugene Bible College (now New Hope Christian College) in Eugene, Oregon.

Terry and Suzette started New Life Foursquare Church in Grand Forks, ND in August 1985. The church began to move in deliverance ministry in December of 1996 as God began to set people free from demonic oppression.

In the Spring of 1997 Terry became involved with Cleansing Stream, a Deliverance ministry centered on discipleship. As of the writing of this book, Terry has been involved in 121 retreats, 100 of which he personally led.

In 2002, the Lord led Terry back to the world of education. He began taking master-level classes at The King's University founded by Pastor Jack Hayford in 2002. Terry earned a Master of Divinity degree in 2006 and a Doctorate of Ministry degree in 2009.

Terry also taught online at The King's University for seven years and is currently and online instructor at Shiloh University in Kalona, IA.

Terry's passion and purpose is to help you experience life as God intends it to be. The work you hold in your hand is the result of God working in his life over the past 40 years.

# Spirit Baptism

The Baptism with the Holy Spirit is one of the central teachings of John the Baptist, Jesus, and the early church. It is described as a gift from God, the promise of God, and an empowering from God. This is something that Jesus wants to pour out upon every believer. He is the Baptizer with the Holy Spirit.

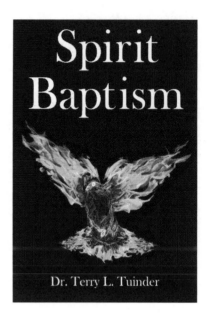

The purpose of this book is to help ordinary believers enter into the fullness of the Holy Spirit. In Acts chapter 2 Peter repeats the promise of the prophet Joel, "I will pour forth of My Spirit on all mankind."

Are you hungry to receive all that the Lord has made available to you? Do you desire to be overflowing with the life and power of the Holy Spirit? Have you been filled with the Spirit and wonder what happened to you? Do you want to help other people receive this wonderful gift? Spirit Baptism will help clarify and strengthen your understanding of the Baptism with the Holy Spirit.

Here is a look at the chapter titles:

- What it Isn't

- What it Is

- Is it for Today?

- How Does it Fit into God's Plan?

- Why Should I Want It?

- How Can I Receive the Gift?

- How Can I Know I've Been Baptized?

- But Do I Have to Speak With Tongues?

- How Long Does it Last?

**Available on Amazon**

# Ploonty Goes to the Moon

## A fun book I wrote with my 10-year-old granddaughter, Trinity

Ploonty is a nine-year-old girl whose imagination runs overtime. Sometimes she thinks so many thoughts she is afraid that her head is going to blow up forcing her to constantly wear a hat so the birds won't eat her brains. Talk about an imagination!

One evening Ploonty and her family are speeding down the road in her father's 1965 souped-up Mustang convertible. Her dad mentions how beautiful the moon is that night, but Ploonty cannot see it from the backseat. Her dad stops the car, lets the car's roof down, and Ploonty captures a glimpse of the moon that changes her life forever. Right then and there, she determines that she is going to go to the moon, and she is going to go sooner not later.

Will Ploonty make it to the moon? Does the moon taste like cheese? Did the cow really jump over the moon? What does the man on the moon look like, anyway? How much will you weigh on the moon? How far can you jump on the moon? Want answers to these and many more questions? Then Ploonty Goes to the Moon is the book for you.

For kids of all ages.

For the full story and pictures of Trinity go to:

http://www.ploonty.com/story-behind-ploonty/

**Available on Amazon**

# Experiencing His Victory Academy

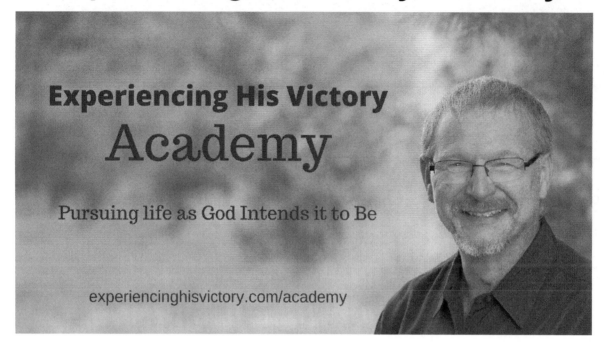

The EHV Academy has three levels of access, both free and paid. It is a one-stop source for all of the materials released through exxperincinghsivictory.com over the years. It includes the following:

- The Free Membership

    - 700+-page PDF Library

    - Access to all free video courses

    - Access to a free Facebook group

- The Paid Memberships

    - Free access to all paid courses

    - Live monthly training (or recordings of the training)

    - Live monthly Q&A session (or recordings of the sessions)

    - Free Premium Facebook group

**experiencinghisvictory.com/academy**